DEVSTREAMS

SCALING SOFTWARE DELIVERY.
NATURALLY.

Yaron Perlman

ISBN: 979-8-38-783423-3

Published by YP Technologies & Consulting Inc.
www.devstreams.com

TABLE OF CONTENTS

PREFACE

This book is by no means theoretical, and the paradigm I will present here is not theoretical either. This book is a practical one, and it offers a very practical approach; thus, for one to get value and be successful with this paradigm, one needs to practice it. Hopefully, reading this book will give you the initial set of guidelines for practicing this paradigm.

Looking at nature and presenting ideas within this book, I am trying as much as possible to take inspiration from what I see in nature in every aspect that I write about and am introducing. Nature has been quite successful in creating a beautiful and long-lasting reality for all of us to benefit from. There must be a way to be successful at understanding the problems that nature has solved. And not only understanding them but taking that knowledge and applying it in an elegant and very useful way. By adopting concepts that nature uses to solve a problem, we get a bonus: the solution feels natural and is usually easier for us to implement. And there are inherent benefits that flow from that; things go together better, they "seem to fit," and strange but beautiful synergies suddenly appear that were not present before. There is truly a grand design to the universe, and by exploring and embracing this new approach, we can tap into that.

When we, humans, try to solve problems, we typically rely on theory and knowledge in the domain of the problem. And that naturally places us "in a bubble" or in a "vacuum" where we can get too close to it and not see things for what they are. The solution usually has a rigorous foundation and an aspect of "completeness" that we can envision or imagine in our minds end-to-end. So, the solution does not evolve as it should; rather, it is presented as a whole.

With this book, I'm attempting to promote an approach similar to how nature creates something from nothing and grows into something original and bountiful. It does so by embedding the fundamental elements within something from which the creation emerges, whether a seed or a cell, the most fundamental element that contains the building blocks and know-how for production through a timely process.

In the same way, view this book as a seed. By absorbing and immersing your mind in it, you will plant the seed, water it, watch it grow, and cultivate it. As you tend to and nurture it, the seed will grow into a beautiful plant. In the same way, what grows out of this book for your benefit will evolve over time and, hopefully, become a new way of doing your work.

You'll notice that some of the topics in this book are presented succinctly. Throughout the book, I tried to communicate and share my ideas by providing the raw essentials of the concept with just the right amount of words to describe it. I've tried to present the concept in itself without unnecessary descriptions around it. If there is more to add, these would probably be subjective, and you could learn these as you practice. The fundamental idea is given; feel free to find your own ways to refine it and personalize it for whatever purpose when needed. You could find ways to make it more meaningful. You could find ways to embrace it, make it your own, and let that idea grow. As well, this is the first edition of DevStreams, and based on reader feedback, additional research, and real-world examples, the second edition may very well be expanded. Stay tuned!

So, as you read the book, you're welcome to skip ahead if you like. Don't feel obligated to follow the order in which the topics are introduced. I do encourage you to look at all of them and at least consider embracing all pillars as one practice. That is definitely how I intended the work to be adopted. All the pieces go together to form one complete practice.

However, my guiding principle is that there are no rules. Keep doing whatever works for you, and you may take it in any direction that provides positive results for your work or project. That is the ultimate goal here. I am trying to introduce a paradigm that produces results and addresses a challenge that today is quite fundamental. The way to get these results is simply to put it into practice. Practice the paradigm, make it your own, dwell on it, contemplate it, try it, tweak it, and experiment with it. I see this as a collaborative effort, and I welcome your ideas as well.

I truly hope you will see something beautiful growing from your experience reading DevStreams. And its fruits are going to be so tasty!

PART 1
INTRODUCTION

THE INSPIRATION BEHIND DEVSTREAMS

The overview of biomimicry provided in chapter 3 aims to support the reasoning behind the inspiration for the DevStreams paradigm presented in part II of the book. The examples we shall look at for biomimicry were largely inspired by the structures and dynamics of living organisms here on earth. To that end, it would be beneficial to explore this subject in a bit more detail. So, let's take it further.

The natural world is a supersystem with varying degrees of complexity that change over time based on structure, function, and interconnectedness with natural life phenomena. Biology, the scientific study of life, is just the tip of the iceberg in terms of inspiration we can draw from the multi-layered dynamics and complex structures we find in nature.

Let's take an archeological tell as a metaphor. In an archeological tell, we typically find stratified debris from multiple settlements at the same site - the relics of generations of people who built and inhabited them. The deeper we dig, the farther back in time we go. By observing the various settlements, we can get a window into a particular moment in time. It's a fascinating way to see what may have happened here on earth a long time ago.

Similarly, nature devises structures and dynamics that produce and sustain life elements in ever-increasing complexity levels. Six main chemical elements make up the fundamental building blocks of living organisms on earth. The two most common are carbon and hydrogen, so a mechanism in nature that helps control the distribution of these chemical elements must deeply impact the life forms that are made of them. You see where this is going, right? It leads us directly to rivers and streams! And rivers and streams are the real inspiration for DevStreams and the methodology we're exploring here.

While it is evident that rivers play a key role in controlling water distribution, a 2014 study reveals that rivers help regulate the global carbon cycle. In this study, published in the industry journal Nature, scientists from the Woods Hole Oceanographic Institution claim that one of nature's methods for the long-term storage and removal of carbon is via the world's complex river system.

"The world's rivers act as Earth's circulatory system, flushing carbon from the land to the ocean and helping reduce the amount of carbon that returns to the atmosphere in the form of heat-trapping carbon dioxide," states lead author and geochemist Valier Galy.

"Some of that carbon—'new' carbon—is from decomposed plant and soil material that is washed into the river and then out to sea. But some of it comes from carbon that has long been stored in the environment in the form of rocks— 'old' carbon—that have been eroded by weather and the force of the river."

Do you see what I am getting at? Rivers and streams carry the burden of sustaining living organisms; they are a deeper layer in our metaphoric archeological tell of existence. So based on that, let's dig a little deeper.

The familiar signature fractal pattern rooted in branching intrinsic to rivers and streams is common to other natural phenomena involving movement and flow. I started working on the fundamentals of DevStreams during a long business trip. At that time, I had already completed the backbone of the practice. It was a hot summer day on my flight back home, and as the plane flew over the islands of Greece, I happened to look out the window at the Mediterranean Sea. I'm not sure about you, but I always try to select a window seat whenever I can when I fly; I enjoy observing the world from a different perspective; a bird's eye view rewards you with important insights.

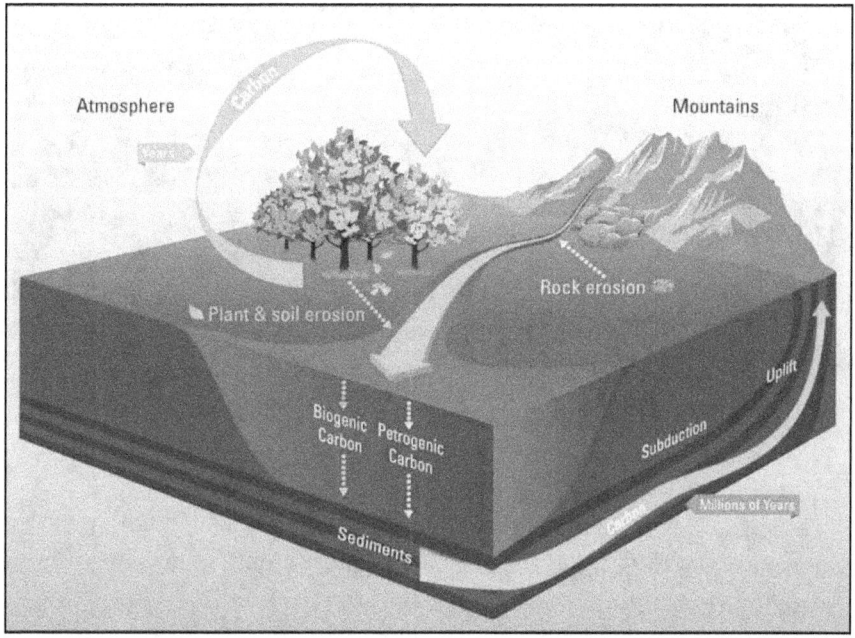

Carbon is a building block for all life and plays a key role in regulating
Earth's climate. It shuttles throughout the planet in two major cycles. [i]

So, as I looked out the window that day, I noticed the familiar structure
of streams emerging from within the ripples of waves from high above.
Seeing rivers of waves flow within the sea reinforced my feeling that I was
on to something big.

And so, I started looking for this signature pattern in other natural
phenomena; as I did, I noticed that it is prevalent almost everywhere we
encounter flow in nature. Let's look at a few other examples through a
series of photos.

The first is an atmospheric river - these rivers in the sky are often
larger than the Amazon, Nile, or the Mississippi and can drive powerful
storms; climate change is making them even bigger and stronger.

Atmospheric river [ii]

Next, we have fractal river-like patterns found in mudflats. Also known as tidal flats, these are coastal wetlands formed from sediments set by tides or rivers.

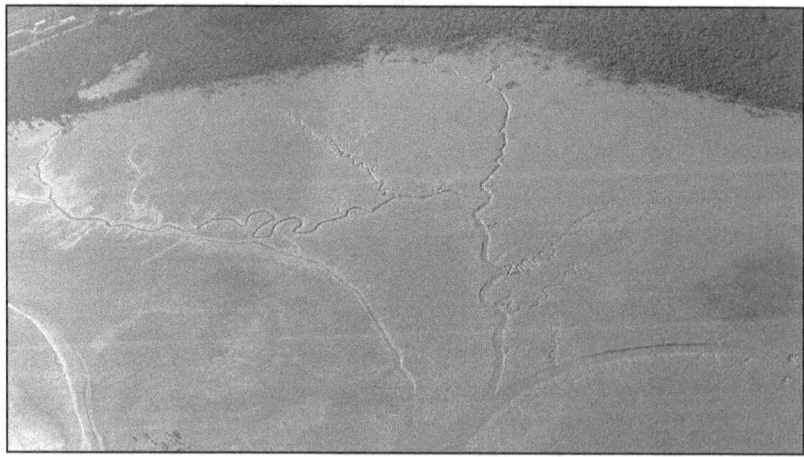

Mangere Inlet – fractal river-like patterns in mudflats [iii]

Lightning bolts also have this fractal branching geometry as the electric charge flows through the air, constantly seeking the path of least resistance.

Lightning bolts [iv]

Rivers flow even in space; NASA's Spitzer Space Telescope captured a rare photo of rivers of stellar gas. PhysOrg.com quotes Matt Povoich of the University of Wisconsin, Madison: *"Powerful winds from the most massive stars at the center of the cloud produce a large flow of expanding gas. This gas then piles up with dust in front of winds from other massive stars that are pushing back against the flow."*

Of course, the laws of physics and mathematics drive this geometry and the signature patterns we observe. Yet, it almost feels like there is something deeper here, an abstract concept that exists on some other level. Believe it or not, this feeling is backed by science. I must admit that I am a fan of Robert Lawrence Kuhn's YouTube channel "Closer to Truth", where he travels the globe searching for vital ideas of existence and discusses profound aspects of our reality with the world's greatest thinkers. I highly recommend checking it out.

Rivers of stellar gas [v]

In a short episode titled "What Things Really Exist?" he poses this question to George Ellis, a distinguished professor of complex systems in the Department of Mathematics and Applied Mathematics at the University of Cape Town in South Africa. Ellis, a "hardcore scientist" by his own account, lists four different kinds of existence we should acknowledge, and I will mention the first two here. The first kind of existence is the world of particles and forces. According to Ellis's philosophy, the second kind of existence is that something must be said to exist if it has a causal effect on the world of particles and forces. It is not just an abstract concept; it has an actual existence.

He gives an example of a Jumbo Jet, which starts as an abstract concept represented through specifications, plan drawings, computer programs, and so forth. The abstract concept of the Jumbo Jet is called, in mathematical terms, an Equivalence Class, and it has a causal effect on the world of atoms and forces because it leads to the existence of an actual object. Software, streams, and rivers are such Equivalence Classes and therefore exist as abstract concepts that feature flow.

Perhaps I'm getting a bit philosophical here, given that this is a practical book, but I think having this understanding is critical. We'll explore the subject in a much more applicable fashion later in the book.

Now on to software delivery…

CHAPTER ONE – SOFTWARE DELIVERY

DevStreams is a paradigm for scaling software delivery. Software delivery is the overarching process of developing software and continuously making it available for users to consume and use. Traditionally, approaches for delivering software were not regarded as one practice.

WATERFALL AND AGILE SOFTWARE DEVELOPMENT

There are various approaches to developing software from a process management perspective. First, we can build software by applying classic project management concepts, which we often call Waterfall - a rigid and structured process with a beginning, an end, and a set of inter-depended activities. Waterfall has been a traditional way of developing software.

The Waterfall methodology is a sequential development process that flows like a waterfall through all project phases (analysis, design, development, and testing, for example). Each phase is completed before the next phase begins.

It follows the adage to "measure twice, cut once." The success of the Waterfall method depends on the amount and quality of the work done on the front end, documenting everything in advance, including the user interface, user stories, and all the features' variations and outcomes.

With the majority of the research done upfront, estimates of the time needed for each requirement are more accurate, and this can provide a more predictable release date. If parameters change along the way with a Waterfall project, it's harder to change course than with the Agile methodology.

Then, there is the contemporary way, the Agile way. Agile focuses on developing software through a continuous and essentially endless process of iterations. These iterations are called "sprints." Sprints have a predefined timeframe, usually two to four weeks. Next, a collection of tasks or stories is selected to focus on within a sprint. During the sprint, these stories go through the standard lifecycle phases: development, testing, deployment, and so on. When we finish one sprint, we continue to the next and then the one after. Continuously.

Agile enables us to create and respond to change. It is a way of dealing with and building something in an uncertain environment. The authors of the Agile Manifesto in 2001 chose "Agile" as the label for this concept because that word represented the adaptiveness and response to change, which was critical to their methodology.

Agile answers the questions: What's going on in the environment that you're in today? How can you identify the uncertainty you're facing? And how do you adapt to that as you go along?

Agile software development is more than Scrum, Extreme Programming, or Feature-Driven Development (FDD)[vi] frameworks. It is more than practices such as pair programming, test-driven development, stand-ups, planning sessions, and sprints. Agile software development is an umbrella term for a set of frameworks and practices based on the values and principles expressed in the Manifesto for Agile Software Development and the twelve Principles behind it.

What really separates Agile from other approaches to software development? The focus is on the people doing the work and how they work together. Typically, solutions evolve through collaboration between self-organizing cross-functional teams. There's a big focus in the Agile software development community on collaboration and the self-organizing team.

DELIVERING SOFTWARE TO THE END USER

When the software is built and ready to be used, as with any product, we need to deliver it to the end users so they can use it for their specific needs. The delivery used to be in the form of a physical package, something tangible that you hold in your hand. You would package the software, deliver it to your customers, then either they or you would install it on end-user computers. Since the delivery aspect of software was similar to the delivery of other consumer products, we could enhance the development process to include the packaging stage.

Once the software is developed and tested, you package the code. Back in the day, you would write an installer, then store it on a tape, disk, CD, or whatever prevalent technology was used at the time. When you completed the software packaging, your job was done, and the responsibility was then passed to the user to install and start using it. Then, of course, comes the stage of maintaining and supporting the software. As users utilize your software, they will always run into issues. That is the nature of software used by humans. Users will invariably have questions, and some features may not work correctly, and that's when the support and ongoing changes to the software come in.

Of course, users will have ideas for improvement and new functionality that may or may not get added. These are initiated by the individuals who design the software or from user feedback, suggesting features and changing things. Software is a process; it's not a static or finite object. Over time, sometimes many years, we engage in delivering and perfecting our software. It is an evolutionary process, without a doubt. Any great software has this quality. It is never done; it is always changing, always improving, always becoming. The goal is to make it more and more useful over time for more and more users.

SCALE ~ THE UNSOLVED CHALLENGE

The way we have been approaching software is closely associated with technology; we call the overall realm of software: Information Technology. However, it turns out that software goes far beyond technology, and we can find similarities to the software evolution process in nature, as we have earlier. So, what are we trying to do here? Suggest a new perspective for looking at the ever-going process of software development, delivery, change, and perfection. Furthermore, we are proposing a way to make this process streamlined to allow us to overcome the most significant challenge. This issue, I believe, exists in many fields and industries. Although we are covering just the field of software in this book, the challenge is ubiquitous: **how do we scale software delivery effectively?**

As software development and delivery practices mature, the question of how we do it becomes less important as it doesn't matter if we choose the Waterfall or Agile approach. It can work well either way. The process for developing software overall works well, and we can deliver it efficiently today.

We mentioned making the software available to users in a physical form, which was prevalent decades ago. Today, of course, it's all in the cloud; there is no more physical packaging and delivery; it is all on-demand, available whenever the user wants it. So, the element of packaging and delivery has been dramatically improved. However, software development has mostly stayed the same over the last few decades. We write code, compile it, and build it, but how we package it and make it available to users has changed immensely.

Most software products we now use, at least to some degree, are being served from and often run on the cloud. For those software products that run almost entirely on the end-user device, the way we deliver the software is now different - we typically download the software over the network.

Once we install it, the software usually updates itself automatically as updates become available. So today, developing and delivering software is a more holistic process. It is way more efficient. And made it easier for the user.

The challenge is scale. As the business producing the software grows, scaling the operation is a considerable challenge, especially if that business is thriving. How do you provide more functionality? Increased stability, service continuity, maintained information security, and improved user experience. How do you scale that? How do you ensure that when you have an issue and write an email or raise a support ticket, it gets responded to and addressed promptly? How can we resolve it promptly, whether it be a bug or a potential enhancement? How do we implement new functionality that is a great business opportunity quickly? That is the question.

Maybe there are similar software solutions out there, and we have competitors. That's almost always the case, right? So, in this case, introducing new features in a very timely manner becomes critical. As our software gets more complex and the number of users increases, maintaining a positive user experience, service level, and software availability becomes that much more challenging.

Increasing scale is now our focus. So, we're not talking about how we develop and deliver our software; we already have processes and procedures for that. Instead, we're looking at the problem of scaling. How do we ensure that whatever we plan for and the methods we have in place will still operate well when we scale up?

The quicker and more extensive the scale growth needs to be, the more complex the problem becomes. Today, scaling is the primary challenge needing a reasonable solution set. The good old, straightforward approach is throwing more resources at it! Do we need to develop more functionality? Let's bring in more developers. Do we need better support?

Let's bring on more support engineers. Or let's bring on more technical writers to write more knowledge articles. Sound familiar?

But guess what? That doesn't work. It doesn't work because of one fundamental rule from the field of microeconomics: Scaling is challenging because of the Rule of Diminishing Returns. **The Rule of Diminishing Returns** states that in a production process, as a production factor increases, the total output increases but will reach an optimal output level before it begins to decrease or diminish.

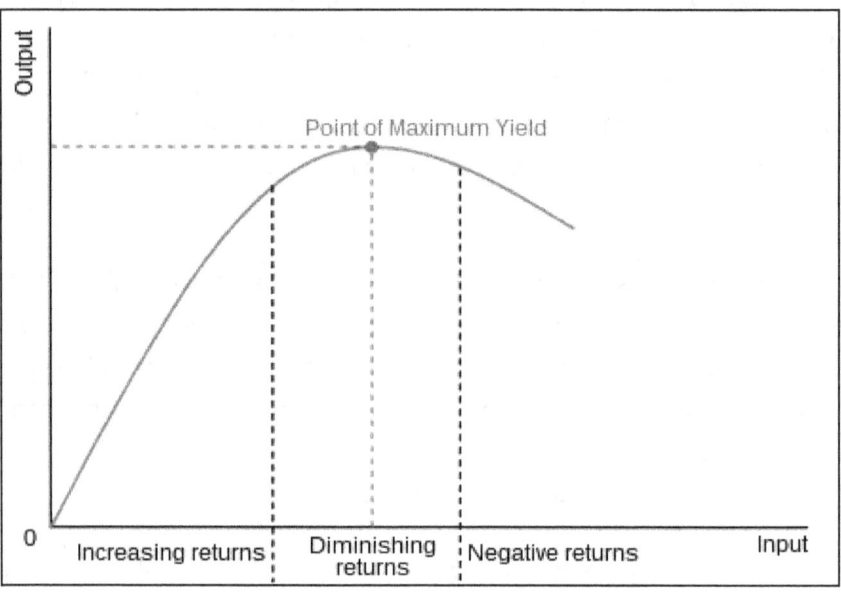

Diminishing Returns Graph: The graph highlights the concept of diminishing returns by plotting the curve of output against input. The areas of increasing, diminishing, and negative returns are identified at points along the curve. There is also a point of maximum yield, which is the point on the curve where producing another unit of output becomes inefficient and unproductive. [vii]

So, the hard fact is that there is a point where adding more resources will start reducing our output. Now that's a rule. It may seem to go against common sense or the natural order, but it actually does make a lot of sense when you think about it. We have all seen the effects of this rule in many areas of life.

How does this play out?

- More resources are tougher to manage; when we make a system bigger, each person focuses on a smaller portion.

- It becomes more challenging to keep individuals engaged; some leave, and we need to replace them - this reduces the output of the rest of the team.

The effects of this rule are evident, and if you look at successful software companies out there, many were able to cope well with the challenge of scaling.

CHAPTER TWO – A FRACTAL NATURE

It's important to know that paradigms and methodologies used to manage software development and delivery were primarily adopted from other fields and disciplines. For example, the Waterfall methodology, invented in the 1970s, was adopted from the waterfall manufacturing method derived from Henri Ford's assembly line innovations.

The Kanban system, a common practice of Agile, was developed for Toyota by Taiichi Ohno, an industrial engineer. Scrum, another successful Agile method, was introduced by Jeff Sutherland, John Scumniotales, and Jeff McKenna at the Easel Corporation. They drew these concepts from the Harvard Business Review (HBR) article – "The New New Product Development Game" (1986), where Takeuchi and Nonaka introduced new approaches inspired by the Rugby sports game.

But the challenges of software development and delivery are unique. Software is a dynamic process that entangles rapid and frequent changes and enhancements. Moreover, unlike any other industry in our modern age, software is developed and delivered by manual labor; it is, in many senses, a "hand-crafted" thing. These unique characteristics largely contribute to the challenge of scale that we are discussing. How do you scale something that is hand-crafted? It merits a new paradigm unique to software that draws inspiration from a similar realm where complexity, change, and scale play a leading role - nature.

Let us explore the phenomena of flowing water in nature. A river is a perfect example of scaling; it enables water flow scaling, right? Water needs to flow from one place to another, and it has to flow effectively, continuously, and in increasing volumes across a great distance. Water must flow to sustain life. It is impossible to imagine any large ecosystem without flowing water being a part of it. So, nature has devised a way to make water flow efficient and scalable.

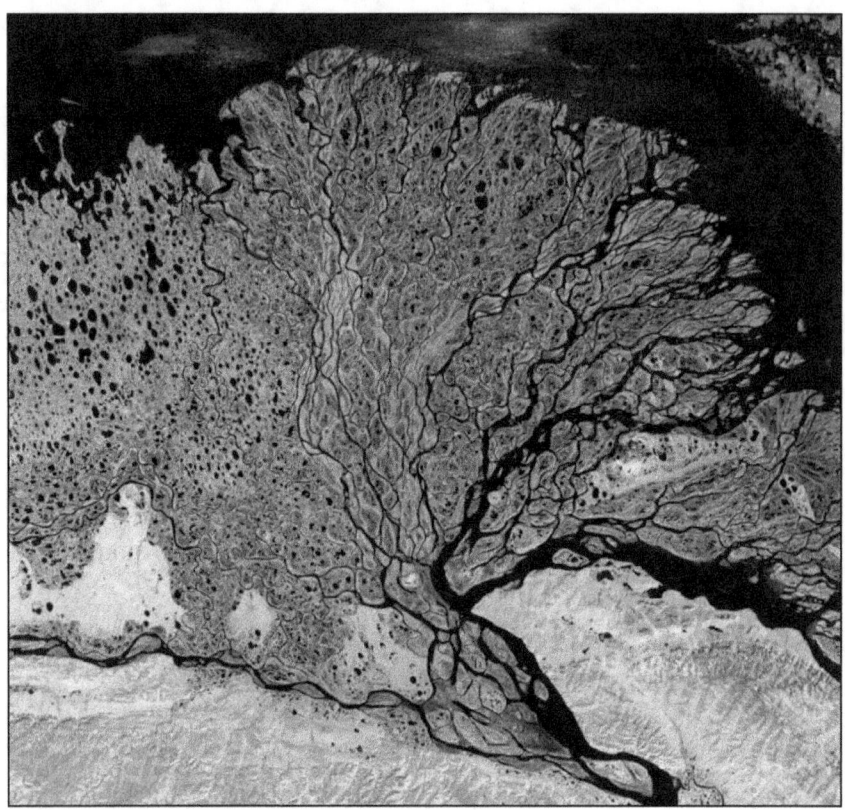

This stunning image, taken on July 27, 2000, shows the Lena River in Russia, one of the largest rivers in the world, which is some 2,800 miles (4,400 kilometers) long. The Lena Delta Reserve is the most extensive protected wilderness area in Russia. It is an important refuge and breeding ground for many species of Siberian wildlife.[viii]

Nature applies a combination of process and structure at varying scales to solve a myriad of problems related to flow at their core. Study the image above. With a river, scale is increased or reduced by splitting and merging the same fundamental design. The result of this self-similarity over varying scales is a particular form of geometry - fractal geometry. Fractal geometry is a branch of Mathematics and Chaos theory; the Polish-French mathematician Benoit Mandelbrot introduced the concept and its applications in his book The Fractal Geometry of Nature (Mandelbrot, 1982).

In mathematics, a fractal is a geometric shape containing detailed structure at arbitrarily small scales. Usually, they have a fractal dimension strictly exceeding the topological dimension. Many fractals appear similar at various scales, as illustrated in successive magnifications of the Mandelbrot set. This exhibition of similar patterns at increasingly smaller scales is called self-similarity, also known as expanding symmetry or unfolding symmetry; if this replication is exactly the same at every scale, as in the Menger sponge, the shape is called affine self-similar. Fractal geometry lies within the mathematical branch of measure theory.

One way fractals differ from finite geometric figures is how they scale. Doubling the edge lengths of a filled polygon multiplies its area by four, which is two (the ratio of the new to the old side length) raised to the power of two (the conventional dimension of the filled polygon). Likewise, if the radius of a filled sphere is doubled, its volume scales by eight, which is two (the ratio of the new to the old radius) to the power of three (the conventional dimension of the filled sphere).

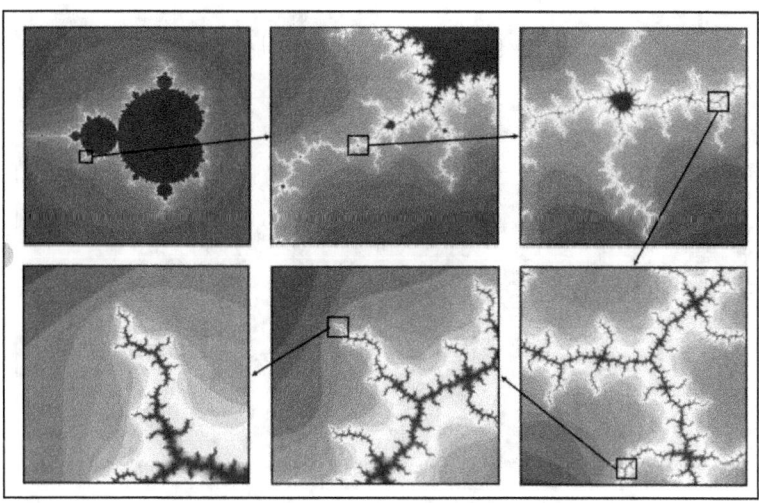

Self-similarity of Mandelbrot set in different scales. [ix]

In nature, energy efficiency is crucial - high-performing structures are created with minimal material and information. Self-similarity enables nature to use the same minimal rules on all scales and achieve an impressive ratio between the amount of information put into the system and the complexity of the outcome. Fractals are everywhere in nature: the branching of a tree, the veins of a leaf, mountain ridges, rivers, the structures of vegetables, and the bronchial structure of the lungs, to name a few.

Close-up view of a leaf structure. [x]

Fractal Patterns in Nature. [xi]

Fractal patterns in trees. [xii]

Natural fractal patterns on earth, viewed from space. [xiii]

Romanesco Broccoli. [xiv]

So why not learn from nature and apply similar concepts, structures, and dynamics to the realm of software delivery? After all, it is only natural! Moreover, it feels right. I believe that our human feelings are the result of hypercomputations that are perceived in our minds. These computations are not the type we were taught in school, not even the kind of computations that computers run or even the ones we now call AI or Deep Learning. There is a recipe for all of these types of computations mentioned above.

So, there is a process when we learn how to divide and multiply numbers in elementary school. There is a structured method; there is an algorithm. This is how modern computers work: they are equivalent to a Turing Machine and run algorithms.

But there seem to be other ways to compute, right? We have little to no understanding of how these computations work, but we are aware of them constantly as they occur in our minds. Think about it.

Our minds leverage a more powerful computation model, and our feelings result from these computations. When we say: "I have a gut feeling" about something, or "it feels like it's the right thing to do," or "I have a good feeling about it,"; all of these terms that we use relate to a computation process that our mind produces and results in a feeling.

We feel the result. So, what happens is that we process numerous parameters that consider a myriad of factors, factors we need to be made aware of. These computations are unique; they are not objective. The processing of information that occurs in our minds is very subjective. I may have a good feeling about something, but my friend may not have such a good feeling about it, or maybe an unpleasant feeling because his mind is trying to tell him it is wrong for him. My mind is telling me this is right for me. And that makes much sense. There is variability between different minds and subjective circumstances.

I will share with you that it felt really good when I thought about this new paradigm and how to solve the scaling challenge of software delivery. It felt like it was the right thing. It felt natural and, in some ways, intuitive. But it wasn't readily accessible. It took some deep thinking and an illuminated imagination. To me, it says that my mind indicates that it is the right way for my particular circumstances. It is a good fit, and it will most probably work. That was the result of the computation that my mind had so elegantly delivered to me. And so, because of this dynamic, I would like to suggest that you don't have to accept the ideas in this book objectively. It has to apply to you and your specific circumstances. It needs to make sense.

So, I encourage you to trust your feelings; if it feels right, then it's probably worth a shot for you to try it; it's probably right for you. And as you continue reading this book, ask yourself; how do I feel about it? Listen to your mind. If you don't feel good about it, your mind is probably trying to tell you it is not a good fit for your circumstance. But then, I would not suggest that you dismiss the idea. Instead, try to find out why it does not feel right, and maybe you can change it. It is now yours; contemplate, mold, transform, and make it right for you; your feeling toward it may change. Things evolve. And sometimes, it all comes together in one clear-eyed moment.

CHAPTER THREE ~ BIOMIMICRY

Much of what I discuss in DevStreams is reflective of the Biomimicry movement, which has been a real thing over the last fifteen years or so. It means "imitation of the living" and takes inspiration from natural selection solutions adopted by nature and translates the principles to human engineering or, in this case, software delivery. After all, shouldn't we favor "choices" and patterns tested by nature, which had millions of years to understand what works best and what doesn't? It's an elegant approach and application to everything we do in life, isn't it?

Designs following biometrics will ultimately allow software development and delivery to be more efficient, resilient, and sustainable, just as nature intended. Survival of the fittest…and the most tried and true approach, right? It seems so elementary and straightforward. But as I mentioned, it's only been a "thing" in the cultural zeitgeist very recently. There is nothing new under the sun unless, of course, you study the sun itself! And the tides, weather patterns, the growth of the Giant Redwoods, and on and on.

BIOMIMICRY INSTITUTE DEFINITION OF BIOMIMICRY

According to the Biomimicry Institute, biomimicry can be defined as "an approach to innovation that seeks sustainable solutions to human challenges by emulating nature's time-tested patterns and strategies. The goal is to create products, processes, and policies—new ways of living—that are well-adapted to life on earth over the long haul."[xv] If I were teaching a university-level class called Introduction to Software Development, I might take my class on a field trip to a zoo or a botanical garden and have the students just observe and take notes. Then apply their observations to a software sprint. Now there's an idea!

THE PRINCIPLES OF BIOMIMICRY, LET'S DIG IN

The "big ah-ha" is that nature has already fixed many issues that software delivery has struggled with. Animals, plants, and microorganisms are experienced engineers themselves! With the help of some almighty force, call it "Universal Energy," they somehow already know what works, what's appropriate for the given situation, and most importantly, what is sustainable on Planet Earth. Shouldn't we just take their example and apply it to human concerns?

Here is the gist: If you are a disciple of the biomimicry approach, you know that after almost four billion years of research and development, what did not work over time is now a fossil, and what is around us everywhere is the secret to survival! And so, it is with software development and delivery. Applied there, we should look at the largest and most successful software platforms on earth and heed their lessons.

Biomimicry is a technological-oriented approach focused on putting nature's lessons into practice. According to Janine Benyus (an American natural sciences writer, innovation consultant, and author; She coined the term Biomimicry), biomimicry sees nature as[xvi]:

- **A model**. It studies nature's models and imitates them or uses them as inspiration for designs or processes with the goal of solving human problems.

- **A measure**. It uses ecological standards to judge the rightness of human innovations.

- **A mentor**. It is a new way of observing, assessing, and valuing nature.

APPLYING BIOMIMICRY TO REAL WORLD SITUATIONS

When you start thinking about the idea of Biomimicry, it truly impacts all areas of human endeavor. From medicine to research, industry, economy, architecture and urban planning, agriculture, and, yes, software…the applications are breathtaking and all-encompassing.

At its core, biomimicry is based on this one big idea: **nature always operates on the principles of economy and efficiency while generating no waste.** The quote, "Nothing is lost, nothing is created, everything is transformed," is attributed to Antoine Lavoisier, who first formulated the law of the Conservation of Mass.

This brilliant observation is comprised of two fundamental concepts that directly impact digital transformation or software development and delivery:

- Transformation
- Conservation

They are fundamental. They must occur at the same pace in any transformation plan because they must be part of the same vision.

No matter the field of application, the biomimetic philosophy is part of a global strategy of responsible and sustainable development that aims to balance the way the planet's resources are used. And the terms "responsible" and "sustainable" also apply to the software sector.

EXAMPLES OF BIOMIMICRY IN NATURE [xvii]

- Climbing pads capable of supporting human weight mimic the biomechanics of gecko feet.

- The aerodynamics of the famous Japanese Bullet train was inspired by the shape of a bird's beak.

- The first flying machine heavier than the air from the Wright brothers in 1903 was inspired by flying pigeons.

- Architecture is inspired by termite mounds to design passive cooling structures.

- Velcro is born from observing the hooks implemented by some plants for the propagation of their seeds via animal coats.

- The study of shark skin is at the origin of particularly effective swimming suits, as well as a varnish for a plane's fuselage.

The nose cone of Japan's 500 Series Shinkansen bullet train
is modelled after a kingfisher's beak. Getty Images [xviii]

ISO STANDARDS AND BIOMIMICRY

Although biomimicry is still an emerging sector, some standards are already backing it up. It's the case of the International Organization for Standardization (ISO) with ISO 18458 (on the terminology, concepts, and methodology) and the standard ISO 18459 (biomimetic optimization). AFNOR, the French national organization for standardization and its International Organization for Standardization member body, also has a standard known as XP X42-502 that focuses on biomimetic and eco-design.

The bottom line? Biomimicry provides an interconnected understanding of how life works, where we fit in, and how we can bring efficiency and scale to software development and delivery. It is a practice that learns from and mimics the strategies used by species alive today. The objective within the greater software paradigm? To create products, platforms, processes, and systems that solve our greatest design challenges sustainably, efficiently, and with less waste.[xix]

Circularity, sustainability, and regenerative design all must be considered when we approach our software challenges. There is something to be learned from all of it. Nature uses structure to change functions and uses passive forms of energy. We can create software conducive to life and the living, just like nature does.

Nature's R&D cycles may seem slow. But all we need to do is look to the biological blueprints that have been successful over millennia to launch groundbreaking software ideas and projects faster. We don't need to reinvent the strategies that exist. It's how we adapt them that counts. It's how we apply them that makes all the difference.

Biomimicry is about valuing nature for what we can learn to inform our software endeavors, not what we can extract, harvest, or domesticate. It's about taking the beauty and bounty of nature and applying principles from nature to every line of code we write and every function of the user experience for maximum impact and benefit.

FUNDAMENTAL COMPONENTS OF BIOMIMICRY [xx]

Nature's strategies require us to translate them into our software designs. To effectively carry that out, we should understand the three essential elements: Emulate, Ethos, and (Re)Connect. These three components are infused in every aspect of biomimicry and represent these core values at their essence. More specifically:

- **Emulate**: The scientific, research-based practice of learning from and then replicating nature's forms, processes, and ecosystems to create more regenerative software designs and delivery mechanisms.

- **Ethos:** The philosophy of understanding how life works and creating software designs that continuously support and create conditions conducive to getting work done.

- **(Re)Connect**: The concept that we are nature and find value in connecting to our place on Earth as part of life's interconnected systems. (Re)Connect as a practice encourages us to observe and spend time in nature to understand how life works so that we may have a better ethos to emulate biological strategies in our software designs. It is the "immersive" approach; to become one with the laws of the universe means we can bring massive improvements in efficiency to our software projects.

An important factor differentiating biomimicry from other bio-inspired design approaches is the emphasis on learning from and emulating the regenerative solutions living systems have for specific functional software challenges.

A KEY DISTINCTION

Let's clear up some confusion. Within the larger scope of bioinspired design, a common misunderstanding is mistaking biomorphism for biomimicry. Biomorphism refers to designs that visually resemble elements from life (they "look like" nature), whereas biomimetic designs focus on function (they "work like" nature). Biomorphic designs can be elegant and inspiring, partly because humans have a natural affinity for nature and natural forms. But it's important to realize that "looking like" nature is not a reliable indicator of biomimetic software design because a biomimetic design might or might not look anything like the organisms that inspired it. Rather, the important indicator is function. It all comes down to how it works and what it does. And how it positively impacts the user.

THE TECHNOLOGIES OF THE NOW AND OF THE FUTURE

So now that we have a firm understanding of Biomimicry and digital naturalness, what technologies should we focus our energies on when it comes to software design and delivery?

In other words, where are the maximum efficiencies gained, and what areas will developers be working in? Artificial intelligence, quantum computing, and the blockchain are all already impacting our lives in big ways but are still early in their development. Let's dig in a bit...

ARTIFICIAL INTELLIGENCE [xxi]

AI is impacting and disrupting fields such as insurance, healthcare, finance, and many others. Much of this technology is "machine learning" based rather than artificial intelligence, which has become an umbrella term covering many ways to make systems smarter.

Two big AI milestones of note: By 2006, facial recognition algorithms were a hundred times more accurate than those from ten years earlier. And then by 2014, Facebook had developed DeepFace, an algorithm capable of recognizing individuals in photographs with the same accuracy as humans.

The original concept of neural networks came from copying, in a simplistic way, how our brain cells interact. And as we now know, biomimicry R&D has expanded to emulate a wider depth and breadth of nature's ways.

What's on the horizon? Improved natural language processing will impact the voice control of many devices, from your smartphone to your kitchen oven. Driverless cars will most likely become the new standard. Detection of most diseases, including cancer, will be done by computers, not doctors. ML usually works best when it recognizes patterns from massive amounts of data.

For an ML-powered self-driving car to be trusted, it's important to understand how it decides what a road sign or a child is. Researchers at MIT have been working on the Transparency by Design Network, which breaks the ML decisions down into smaller modules and visually renders the thought process as it solves each part of the problem, allowing human analysts to understand its decision-making process.

QUANTUM COMPUTING [xxii]

ML and AI are making a big impact, while QC is the next big thing. Physicist Paul Benioff proposed a quantum mechanical model of the Turing machine forty-two years ago and was clearly ahead of his time. Why is QC so exciting? It has the potential to do calculations that would take today's computers thousands of years. That's a big deal.

As we know, today's computers, at their base level of operation, use a "bit" which can be 0 or 1; a QC uses a "qubit," which can be either of those or a superposition of both 0 and 1. So, in essence, computers today are set up to provide a yes or no answer. A QC can make calculations with answers which include yes and no, maybe, or both, etcetera.

A powerful QC will open up the possibility to simulate fluids accurately, molecule behaviors, protein folding – lots of revolutionary, never before done things. This will result in a mountain of technological breakthroughs, from new materials to the invention of new medical therapies and many other things not even conceived of yet.

QC's today have less than 200 qubits. To be useful, QC needs many thousands of qubits, so as you can imagine, there is lots of R&D going on. IBM and Google have major projects in motion, and there are now a few exciting startups going after it as well. Stay tuned!

BLOCKCHAIN ^{xxiii}

Blockchain has been a hot topic for a while now. Many believe it will be as disruptive as the Internet itself when all is said and done. Distributed finance (DeFi) built on top of blockchain technology will transform the financial sector. From changing the way financial entities are created and governed to accelerating services for the unbanked, the financial industry is the world's largest worth $20 trillion annually.

Decentralized applications (dApps) are being built mostly on Ethereum (ETH) and are already changing how organizations operate. Decentralized autonomous organizations (DAOs) are attempting to make decision-making decentralized and automated, using rules encoded as a computer program or smart contracts in blockchain speak, which are controlled by the organization members, which could be many thousands of people. These are very early in their development but could have a massive impact on future commercial organizations, NGOs, and even governments.

All three of these technologies will revolutionize the world around us, industry by industry, product by product, and serve as a tectonic shift in how we all live. DevStreams will be all about these three over the coming years. But what exactly is the paradigm? What is the first pillar in this practice that I'm proposing?

On to PART 2!

PART 2
THE DEVSTREAMS
PARADIGM

CHAPTER FOUR –
THE PARADIGM AND THE FIRST PILLAR

In previous chapters, we talked about the challenge of scale in software delivery, and we have introduced the Law of Diminishing Returns as the principal reason for the challenge of scaling up value delivery. We also established that nature had devised a way to scale efficiently and specifically around the challenge of flow and maximizing energy efficiency to information ratio, or in other words, using minimal information to achieve high energy efficiency with complex outcomes.

So yes, nature has been highly successful in scaling, and not only here on Earth, by the way. Pictures from Mars taken by probes reveal the same type of structure for streams and rivers. So, it is safe to say that it's not only on Earth that nature devised a way to scale delivery; it looks like at least the same concepts and structures are used throughout the solar system. It's a "universe thing". An elegantly designed, super-structured methodology that we see across the cosmos.

It is now time to present the paradigm and the practice. Over the following chapters, we will apply the concepts, structures, geometry, and dynamics in software delivery. Are you ready?

The first rule of the practice is <u>that there are no rules</u>, which is a rather important rule. I was debating whether this should be the first or last rule, and I came to the conclusion that it made sense for it to be the first rule. It may appear as though it doesn't have to do much with the nature of the practice, but it is an integral aspect of how we should adopt it; it is the DNA of the practice. So, there are no rules.

Next, I will provide guidelines for the practice, the pillars of the practice, which are ideas and techniques for adopting various aspects and behaviors we see in nature. Note, though, that as we frequently see, there is no cookie-cutter approach here. Although it may sound counterintuitive, there is no objectivity in anything we see in nature, or anywhere in the universe for that matter. A revelation, for sure! See, everything depends on the point of view of the experience and is very subjective to that point of view. This rule is very important, and for this reason, I would like to suggest that any pillar we present here should **undergo a form of adjustment, modification, or refinement by you, the reader**. Sound good?

Make every pillar your own. Contemplate what it means for your context and understand the rationale at its root. By no means should you follow it without question; regard it as potential, and from that potential, realize what's suitable for your scenario. You see, you may need to slightly change some pillar elements, or you could simply reject the pillar entirely. Not all the pillars will make sense for what you are working on. You can disregard whatever does not fit your reality and the challenges you are experiencing.

This could be something you do over time: Perhaps you start with a minimal set of pillars if there is a challenge in implementing all of them at once. Others may elect to begin implementing all the pillars simultaneously. If they encounter obstacles, they contemplate them and experiment with variations to see if they can clear them away. So that is truthfully the first rule: **Don't accept all pillars as one monolithic technique**. Experiment and make it your own; adjust, tweak, and mold it to your reality. That's the way of human nature anyway! And we are all a part of nature; let's not forget that.

The first pillar we shall introduce is the one we physically see in terms of structure when we observe the phenomena of flow in nature through streams and rivers. This pillar is about the software delivery fundamental unit, similar to the concept of energy quantum in quantum physics - the quantum of software delivery is the *Stream*.

Nature is not continuous. Everything in our reality has a fundamental quantum. There is an energy quantum and a time-space quantum. Anything that we can measure in our universe has an irreducible quality - The same applies to software delivery. We have a quantum. It is the minimal and irreducible unit we leverage when delivering software - the Stream. It is interesting, isn't it, that the fundamental unit is not a single resource or an individual? Think about that one.

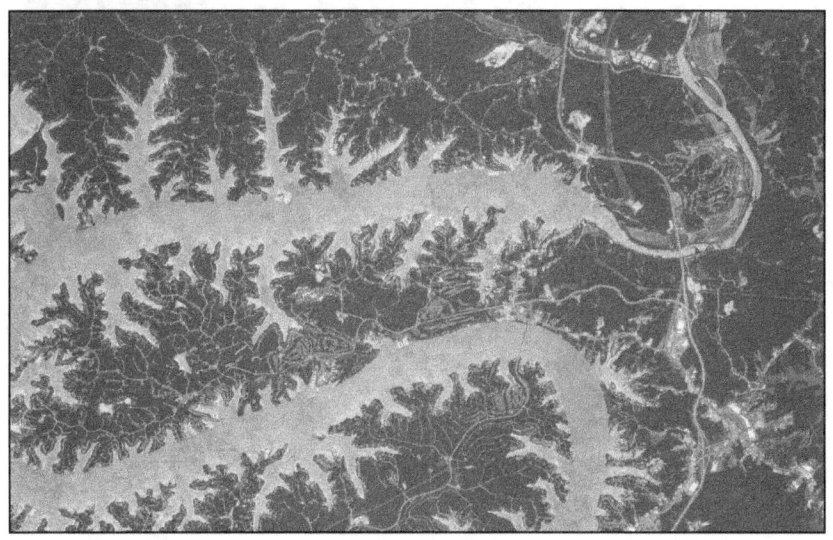

Lake of the Ozarks in Missouri is pictured from the International
Space Station as it orbited 261 miles above the Midwestern United States. [xxiv.]

A stream has two to seven members. Two to seven members is the sweet spot for software teams. Where things can get messy is the eighth beyond seven members (and again, no rules!). From my experience, the effects of the Rule of Diminishing Returns become significant when you go beyond seven individual resources. A delivery unit of two to seven is that optimal set of resources beyond which we start seeing those adverse effects, and the challenges of working with multiple resources become evident. So, the stream is a quantum - the fundamental unit of delivery.

Seven is the upper limit regarding the number of members in a stream. Two is the minimum, beyond which we don't have a stream as we are down to a single resource. During the coming chapters, as the processes and techniques are outlined, you will develop a feel for why a single resource does not embody or define a stream. But for now, since we have already discussed flow, think of flow in terms of dynamics. This form of dynamics typically requires at least a duo.

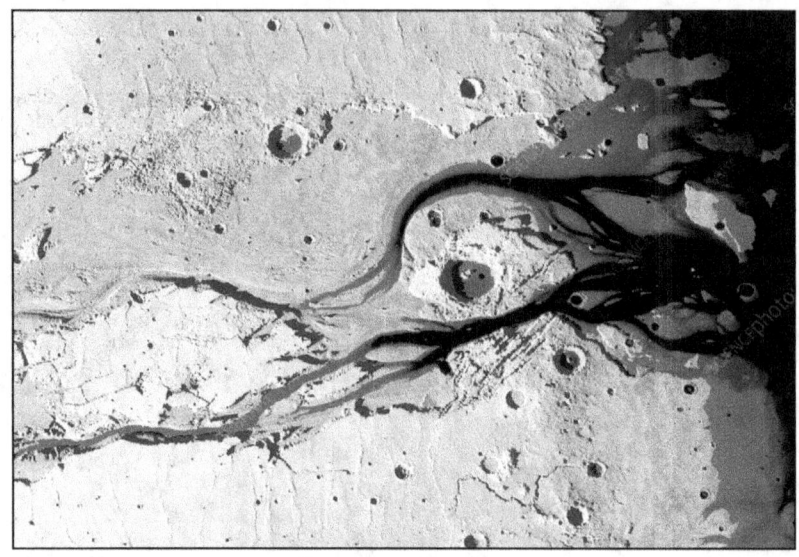

Rivers on Mars.[xxv]

Focusing now on the structure of a stream in terms of skills, responsibility, and proficiency, what does the internal organization of a stream look like? This is where it becomes even more interesting. When we look at traditional software delivery organizations, teams are usually arranged by uniform proficiency, a given facet of the overall software organization.

So, for example, we would have teams for back-end development, then front-end development or UX teams. Then, we would have data and data scientist and product management teams.

In DevStreams, this is different. The stream, as we have said, is the quantum. It must contain all the aspects, a rainbow, the spectrum of all proficiencies and specialties we find in a software organization. Adding to that is the notion of uniformity as we focus on the structure. Uniformity is the third characteristic of the stream, where the members have all the various proficiencies and skills required to deliver software.

Edward Burtynsky, Colorado River Delta #2, Near San Felipe, Baja, Mexico, 2011. [xxvi]

In a stream, everyone does everything. It doesn't mean that everyone is at an expert level in any aspect of software; that is not a fair requirement. Each member of a stream is stronger in one or more aspects of software delivery, but everyone is involved in all the value aspects of the stream. Everyone does DevOps, everyone does QA, everyone does functionality coding, and everyone does data and UX. Everyone does support and customer care, knowledge, and documentation. Everyone does everything.

Well, you may say: "But this doesn't really make any sense to me. Some of these proficiencies are extremely specific, a doctrine, a matter of education and experience, a career path". And that may be right; you may have something there, but if you contemplate this further, there are typically many commonalities for all members of a successful software organization. Code and the skill of coding, for example, are used almost anywhere: in automated testing, DevOps, and data science; it is just the context, methodology, and details that change, but these can be shared and passed on between the members. And this idea is true for all stages and skill sets in the software organization.

Let's take another facet as an example, something that requires creativity and is fundamentally foreign to software delivery: Graphics.

Say the stream needs to deliver a particular component with graphic design requirements and a visual element. Graphics roles typically require a different skill set than software roles; how would you get other stream members to provide value in a graphics portion of the project? Well, there are always tasks that you can teach and let other members perform, right? This aspect of uniformity is highly beneficial because anyone in the stream can perform almost any job.

And here is the magic. We see it in nature, and we see it in software: **Uniformity leads to diversity in day-to-day activities and positive dynamics between members, which quickly translates to increased efficiency**. In the past, what I found challenging in my work was often having to do the same thing over and over again; I would come in and do the same type of work repeatedly, and I was over-saturated and worn out. In all human endeavors, there's clearly a saturation point where you start to lose interest in what you do; the quality of your work diminishes, you begin operating as if you were on autopilot, and as a result, you pay less attention. Right? We can all relate to that. And when this happens, you focus on other things in your mind, and overall, the quality of your work output is different. Unintended results manifest. Software users will see it.

Your mind ultimately starts wandering unintentionally; it looks for other things to focus on, and it becomes more challenging to keep it engaged. Having that diversity, a rich daily experience, and looking at the same things from different angles and points of view opens up your world and gives you a broader perspective. It may run counter to how some individuals operate, but it's a very important point.

Tying the Stream concept to biomimicry and biological metaphors, in "Bioteaming: A Manifesto For Networked Business Teams", Ken Thompson argues that: *"The team is in itself a super-organism, and as such it needs to be treated in ways that enhance and support its complex and interconnected nature. If you can see the team as a whole and not as the mere aggregation of the individual parts that make it up, you can discover how much more productive, reliable, and efficient a virtual team can be."*

This type of team structure is perhaps rare, but certain aspects of what I have outlined as the characteristics of a stream exist, and oddly enough, my first job was in an organization of this sort. My first team member experience delivering software was in a unit similar to a stream structure. It was almost thirty years ago, in the early nineteen nineties. And while I can't talk specifically about what we did because it was in the Israeli Defence Forces, the essence of what we developed was trainers, computer-based training, and trainers.

It was a unique department. We were working with Mac computers, and it was cutting edge at that time in the true sense of user experience. The visual user interface, graphics, and audio capabilities felt out of this world! Before that generation of Apple computers, you needed much imagination, if you are old enough, you probably remember the minimalistic graphics and lack of visuals back in the nineteen seventies and eighties. Computers had the "green screen" experience text-based user interface in those days. It was the first time I experienced computer-based multimedia; it felt futuristic. That department developed advanced trainers, and by the way, exciting start-ups came out of that department.

In that department, the organizational structure was such that they had a single dedicated team responsible for each trainer. A team handled all the trainer's aspects: implementation code, graphics, visual and audio effects, simulation model, and various trainee behavioral aspects. So, there would be a subject matter expert for the realm the trainer was developed. There would be a product designer (we call it a product manager nowadays). The development team also handled packaging and delivery aspects.

Let's explore an example at this point that illustrates the first concept we introduced and demonstrate how we can break the rules regarding the three characteristics of a stream. If we take the teams in my department and see them as streams, then that team would not have been holistic. Why? Because there was a "full-time" stream core made of coders, a graphic designer, and a subject matter expert. In addition, the product manager was separate from the integral team and worked with several groups, dedicating a portion of his time to each product. Teams, however, did own various aspects of the overall design and functionality; they had a free hand to do so under the guidance of the product manager.

There was actual cross-domain ownership. The uniformity aspect was undoubtedly there, the part where everyone does everything. For example, in the team I was part of, I did a lot of the graphics work, handled scanning and image refinements, and learned to work with various graphics editing software. I also did some of the quality assurance and was let into much of the details of coding and implementation.

Ultimately, I transitioned to a lead product role from a subject matter expert. It is another example of how Stream members transition from being an expert on one subject to being an expert in another, leading to a diverse aspect of the team and an overall feeling of contribution and self-fulfillment for each team member.

Let's summarize: the first pillar of the paradigm is that the stream is a software delivery quantum. It has two to seven members. Everyone does everything; there is a dedicated expert for each subject matter of the stream, but they all work together as one unit. Okay good!

What's next? The idea of liberty...

CHAPTER FIVE – LIBERTY: TWO FACETS

The next pillar of DevStreams has two facets that embody an important construct, a fundamental component of living that has been the aspiration of countless humans throughout history. These facets are Autonomy and Accountability; in my mind, these are the two key components of Liberty.

Liberty, as they say, has no price. Liberty in an organization or your work doesn't mean you can do whatever you wish. Rather, liberty allows you to do things you typically can't do when you don't have that freedom. Liberty can also provide you with a distinct and unique state of mind that allows you to accomplish more than you would have in the absence of that state of freedom. Everyone needs to have some level of personal control if they want to accomplish big things.

AUTONOMY

The first facet, Autonomy, for the sake of our discussion here, expresses that a stream has a form of independence, which I call Min-dependence; it is a minimal dependence on other streams, similar to the loosely coupled approach in software architecture. We have stated in the first pillar that the Stream is a quantum and contains all the elements required to deliver value, but this does not mean that a stream operates in a void. There is a natural interdependency.

A stream is a part of the software organization and works in conjunction with other streams. Streams share the same landscape but have distinguishable boundaries for the functionality they deliver and the resources they use. The idea behind minimal dependence is that if the operation of one stream is degraded, the effect on the other stream should be minimal. For example, consider a stream that centers around delivering the Business Intelligence aspect of a product. This stream utilizes an independent data management platform fed by ETL jobs.

Suppose a stream handling the operational data experiences a service degradation; the effect on the BI stream should be minimal as it uses its own data management platform and, ideally, its own set of foundation services. Thus, the impact would be limited to data currency, while the BI services would still be available. Make sense?

Simulated landscape using multiple programs. [xxvii]

Autonomy is the freedom to decide on the various aspects of the stream. For example, if we look at the technology stack, this is where the stream can exercise its autonomy. The stream is free to choose the dev-stack to be used to deliver value. So, if the stream members like using Node.js, they use that; if they prefer .Net, Java, or a Python-based stack - they choose that.

Whatever the stream decides on and agrees to, that will be the dev-stack tech they will use and leverage. The same goes for processes: If they like the Agile methodology, they'll go Agile, and they can choose whether it's Kanban, Scrum, or something else. They are free to choose their delivery processes. They get to shape their own culture and working environment - some streams will work remotely, and others prefer working in an office setting; it can also be a hybrid model. Whatever works best for the individual and the overall team is the best course of action.

So, the streams have the freedom of choice; they are in charge of their own cultures and have that liberation of operating within an environment that feels comfortable and allows them to maximize their delivery potential, just as streams do in nature.

ACCOUNTABILITY

The second facet of Liberty, and the counterpart of Autonomy, is Accountability. Since the stream is the quantum, accountability is on the stream level. Typically, in modern organizations, accountability is individually focused - the team leader is accountable, the Director, the VP, and so on. In DevStreams, the stream is a quantum - there is no individual accountability - the entire stream as an indivisible unit is accountable for its operation and what it produces and delivers. If there's a gap, or if something doesn't work well - this is where accountability becomes relevant. In DevStreams, accountability is about driving change, not negative implications, as we have come to equate with the term accountability. This is a key distinction.

We have said earlier that software is a process, not a constant object. It is flowing and evolving all the time. Every process has the aspect of change; it is natural – so this is what we are looking for in its function and operation. We strive to be better all the time, and we do that by measuring ourselves and being accountable for what we do. We have the freedom to choose whatever we do, but if that doesn't work, we change it and make another choice. Accountability and responsibility are catalysts for change.

Breaking down the characteristics of accountability and autonomy has its merit. Still, for our purposes here, it would be more beneficial to talk about the embodiment or how these two facets help drive and maximize an organization's potential. We start by ensuring we are not losing valuable resources when our organization grows; additionally, we want to maximize our return on investment from both the organization's perspective and the individuals that make up our organization. From the organization's perspective, autonomous streams safeguard us from overlooking good candidates as we scale. From the candidate's standpoint, autonomy enables them to explore their abilities, drive themselves to be more effective, and find out within themselves what they were unaware they could operate, produce and achieve.

Let's explore a few examples to illustrate the point. First, let's discuss how we may overlook or miss out on individuals who could be valuable to our organization. It happens all the time and is an unfortunate thing, but it can be minimized. Think about it; technology and dev-stacks are considerable factors in us dismissing one candidate over another. Suppose our organization is predominantly swayed towards a particular technology; we will typically be looking for candidates with an affinity and experience in that technology.

Our underlying assumption is that a candidate may not be a fit for our organization, but having a diversity of technologies empowers each stream to choose its technology stack of preference. Now our organization is open to more possibilities regarding the types of resources and experience we can consider. As a result, the likelihood of missing out on valuable resources is significantly reduced.

Another critical aspect of an organization is culture. Looking at a job listing from a candidate's perspective, company or team culture is a significant deciding factor. I can easily apply this to myself; in looking back over my career, I was never really a good fit for larger organizations. Large enterprises, in my mind, can't truly provide freedom, at least the autonomy I need to do my best work. With past opportunities and at the level I was applying for, I could not be influential the way I wanted.

Being significant and influential in my work and with whom I work has always meant a great deal. Considering a work environment from a cultural perspective, larger enterprises lost me. I lost the opportunity to work in a compelling business climate with exciting technology and other potential positive aspects. Why? Because I wasn't really considering these larger organizations, or I didn't think I was a good fit.

So how do you break down the barrier between large and smaller enterprises? By structuring organizations as streams and giving them autonomy. They're truly all the same, or should be. With this approach, you're always part of a stream and can choose the stream that better suits you from a technological and cultural perspective. Since you have that freedom as a stream member and contributor to the organization, you can fulfill your potential for personal and professional growth. And all is good in the world. And with software!

CHAPTER SIX – INTEGRATE, MUTATE, ITERATE

This pillar plunges into how we produce and deliver value within the stream. When we discuss deliverables in the software world, we talk about the creation process. So how do we create? Thinking about creation is usually associated with innovation and originality. And oddly enough, this is how I believe we are very different than what nature does.

From a subjective point of view, equating creativity with originality makes sense. Expressing yourself creatively leads to self-fulfillment, a sense of accomplishment, and uniqueness that some of us strive for. Creativity is an attribute we typically find in artists, such as painters, poets, and musicians. Still, software is not really about art, and it shouldn't be; it may have artistic elements. However, software is not an artistic endeavor in the way we typically regard creativity; it is more of a science. And science and art are seemingly on opposite poles.

But back to creativity and how it applies to our discussion. I would like to suggest a different way to achieve creativity in production cycles, which is essential because we're talking about a process, after all. When you think of art, a work of art, it's something we create out of nothing, something completely new that we produce. Creativity is tough to define; it is a unique introduction of something that is made from a void. While this is great for art, it is not usually so great for software development. Software development is continuous. It is not the product of an act with a distinct beginning and an end. It is not an object we present in a museum, hang on a wall, or listen to on Pandora. Instead, software is a living creature; it is an evolving process producing value continuously. It is not static like a completed work of art.

We should think of it as a process, a state that evolves as we continue to improve and perfect it.

So, you may ask, how do we start this process? We begin by proposing a different interpretation of creativity within our practice. In DevStreams, we do not create something out of a void; we integrate readily available elements. We do not build software from scratch, a proclivity prevalent amongst many software developers. For various reasons, developers consistently seem to look for ways to reinvent the wheel for the pure sake of reinvention. Of course, they start with some technological foundation, a dev-stack as we call it, but from that baseline, they will build from more or less inception, making scaling difficult. There are exceptions for which an invention is merited, but those are rare.

INTEGRATE

I'd like to suggest that we take a different approach. We look at what nature does to enable the process of continuous growth and continuous delivery. Nature does that by reusing and assembling existing structures and turning them into something new. Therefore, using a biomimicry approach, instead of creating something from a void, you would look for existing elements and then modify and re-assemble them to address your unique requirements. Make sense? In this way, we interpret creativity differently. Creativity stems from researching existing solutions that solve a portion of the needs and repurposing them in a way that works for what we must solve. And in many ways, this is how a book is written; the topic is researched heavily, and many portions of other books and research papers are used to create an original written work. We are now being creative exactly as nature is. We see this all around us. We see mechanisms that work in one organ in one organism; in turn, they get applied to another organism and other species.

The following examples from nature show how a similar structure is reused and integrated over varying scales. The first photo is of a river and streams in Norway taken from space. This structure allows for maximized efficiency of water flow over a given area and supports life across that geographical area. Observing this nested and fragmented pattern with self-similarity, we can see the similarity with the structure of the branches of a tree, and indeed the next photo is of a tree without leaves. Nature is solving again to maximize flow efficiency, but with trees, this pattern helps achieve structural strength and allows the trees to withstand stress. Can you see how this concept could be utilized in your software work?

A similar structure and technique are applied in two very different problem domains, but both share the elements of growth and scale. The third picture is of the lungs bronchial trees of four commonly studied strains of mice. The same pattern and structure of fragmented, meshed self-similar branching of airways are used to maximize air volume and drive energy efficiency in the living organism. The same approach and structure across various strains of the same life form, tree, and river. All products of nature feature process and flow as the central theme. Nature does not invent itself from the void when it stumbles across a new problem; it reuses, integrates, and mutates the same techniques and structures in an iterative process. Elegant and efficient. And we can mimic that.

River and streams in Norway as viewed from space.[xxviii]

Fractal patterns in tree branches.[xxix]

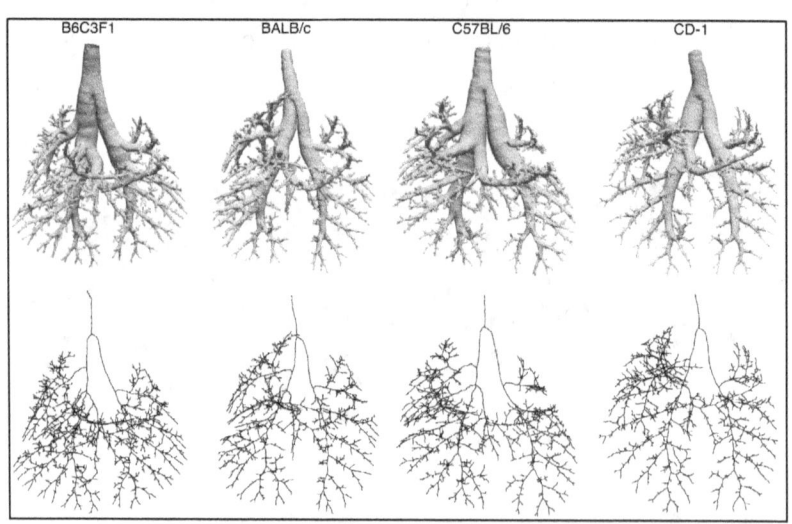

Reconstructed bronchial trees from four different mouse strains.[xxx]

My suggestion? Be creative in assembling and integrating software components rather than being creative at developing from scratch. It's just a better way. And you are still being creative!

I'll share a story from my past as a developer and a development leader. Our story begins in Israel, in the early 2000s, around October of 2000. At that time, my business partner and I had a small team and worked as an independent division within a mid-market systems integrator and security services provider. We operated as the information systems and applications development arm of that organization. These were the early years of the Internet, the .com bubble days, just months before the bubble exploded. A flourishing time of a wealth of applications and content - the New Economy, super exciting times!

One bright morning, through business relations with our CEO, the three founders of TheMarker.com, a leading business newspaper, showed up in our tiny office. They were editors, business news writers, and renowned Israeli newspaper and media industry figures. They formed the vision of the first online business newspaper in the country - this online newspaper was the Israeli subsidiary of TheStreet.com. That morning, they typed in the URL www.thestreet.com in our Netscape Navigator browser as the online newspaper website slowly loaded.

"This is what we need," they said, "and we need it done yesterday." Obviously, we couldn't take our time in a multi-year class endeavor. We were contracted to deliver a fully operational solution and had a few short months to go from basic ideation to full production. This time crunch was part of a tight race with another media group, an enterprise we knew was working on its own version of an online business newspaper.

The three founders each had their area of focus and responsibility; one was technology oriented and led the technical discussions, another was leading the content and desk aspect, and the third ran the operations and project aspects of the endeavor. Together, they were a form of a board of directors, and my partner and I were in charge of delivering the entire project: building and deploying the first online newspaper in the country. A big challenge indeed!

SCALING SOFTWARE DELIVERY. NATURALLY.

I'll refrain from discussing standing up the data center part of the project - connectivity, database, storage and backups, security, web servers, and layer four switches. Those were the days when commercial data centers were unavailable - you had to build and operate them independently. We'll leave all of that aside. Instead, I will focus on how we developed and integrated the software that powered this online newspaper.

We had two options. In those days, the wealth of solutions out there was not abundant. We could either go with the content delivery products global online newspapers used as a driving platform or develop a similar platform ourselves. One of those content management delivery products was Vignette (acquired in 2009 by OpenText), which had representation in Israel then. It was the platform that TheStreet.com used to run its online newspaper. The local Vignette reps were heavily trying to sway us towards using it, but we felt it wasn't a good fit. While it would allow us to fulfill the task of introducing an online newspaper in the short term, it wasn't positioned to be a good fit for the long term.

We didn't feel this was a flexible enough tool for the wealth of requirements we were given and the features that were planned to be a part of this newspaper. Financial tools, online advertising management, third-party content, syndication, and other components were all intended to blend into the platform. As the team responsible for building the solution, we were free to do things the right way. We strongly felt that going with Vignette would not be the right path, and we were fortunate enough to have the full confidence of the founders; they trusted us to go with our gut feeling.

The other option was building the system from scratch, but that would be an endeavor for a team much larger than what we had. And it would take a lot more time, which, unfortunately, we did not have. It was not a viable option. The only remaining option was to introduce something new from existing solutions or applications that were available at the time but didn't fulfill the entire set of requirements. Just as nature does, we would assemble a solution from sub-components that we would then integrate into something new.

One such sub-component of the system was content management, the process of getting an article written by a desk member as a Word document ready to be published. The process involved reviewing draft iterations, rewrites, proofing, and editor reviews until the final version was ready for publishing. This entire lifecycle had to be managed within our system.

We researched a few content management products and found a good candidate, a leading product for creating website content in a structured team environment. That product had a very becoming name: TeamSite. While it was unsuitable for delivering and publishing content on the web, it was a good fit for the content authoring process and the internal desk work.

TeamSite was the component we chose for content authoring. Then we had to mimic and deliver the traditional newspaper's publishing and delivery aspects. How were we supposed to do that? Java was the technology we worked with on our team - the early days of the Enterprise Edition of Java. We needed a foundation for this overarching solution - a delivery platform. In those days, it was called an Application Server, and several were available in the market. We ended up going with the state-of-the-art innovative, and ahead of its time Application Server named Dynamo, developed by ATG - Art Technology Group. ATG developed technologies preceding those out of Sun Microsystems.

Specifically, we leveraged an early version of JSP (Java Server Pages), similar to Microsoft's ASP (Active Server Pages) technology. The Java variant in the Dynamo world was called JHTML; The Java Application Server provided the dynamic aspect of the server-side HTML that preceded JSP technology.

SCALING SOFTWARE DELIVERY. NATURALLY.

It was indeed a marvelous piece of technology. It was scalable, robust, and had the Enterprise readiness to perform as a sound foundation. Dynamo ended up being our choice. It featured applications on top of the platform itself (years before Apple leveraged this concept), which was perfect for us. It felt like the right approach to incorporate additional elements of the required functionality: Ad management, syndication, and third-party content. ATG developed applications for these areas, and although they were not a perfect match for our needs, they at least provided a baseline for us to start from.

Our plan was to integrate Dynamo and TeamSite and to include a complete set of newspaper desk content management, content delivery, and an applications platform for additional aspects of the online newspaper. That was our development strategy. Then, we would focus on developing the integration and customizing the solution's content delivery and other applicative components from a sound baseline. The scope was well outlined, and there was a good balance between proven products and technology and custom development for specific features. We introduced that approach to the owner of the media group - a high-profile type of guy. I am not even sure how we mustered the confidence! Still, my partner presented the solution of choice with conviction, analyzing the other options and building the presentation in a way that favored our approach. It worked!

So just like that, we were given the green light to go ahead with our plan and deliver the working system within five months in spring of that year. And that's what we did. After five months of exceptionally intensive work, literally working around the clock, we stood up a designated data center just in time. We developed the integrated solution, the front-end online paper with a sleek graphic design, the news desk content management, the back-end content delivery systems, ad management, and financial tools. All that wealth of value was delivered in just under two quarters: an operating news desk of over twenty-two writers and a well-oiled information system department that we handed over to that organization for them to continue to operate.

The same foundations remained unchanged for years afterward. So, from my perspective, this is an excellent example of how software delivery takes shape as a live process created by integrating modified components over continuous iteration.

When we discuss creating software by applying the "Integrate, Mutate, and Iterate" approach, I should emphasize that they are equally essential. We shouldn't take each of those as independent building blocks or pick one over the other. The three represent a single tripod concept, and that concept is Evolution. Evolution is a process of continuously selecting small changes over time from a given starting point and applying strategies that work in one realm to another - sounds familiar right?

MUTATE

I'll demonstrate this with another short story I heard from the VP of Engineering in a company I consult. We got to know each other over the years, and I recently shared with him some of the concepts and ideas we have been discussing in this book. I wanted to get his opinion and input. We talked about the creative process around the scenario of integrating a pre-built component into your code set. He shared his insight from their experience introducing a rather complex and functional heavy front-end component with visual and data model aspects into their user interface.

This company has a dominant product management presence, and the product leadership was very involved in selecting that component. They purchased the license to use a component developed by a third party. All through the shopping and assessment, the VP of Product and the strong figures on his team were happy with the functionality of that component. Still, during the initial integration, things started to take a different direction, and product leadership was very keen on changing fundamental aspects of that component's visuals and behavior. These changes were to the point where Engineering said, "well, if that's what you're looking for, it's easier for us to build it from scratch ourselves."

The first thing we can take away from this story is that when we are shopping around for a starting point, we can use the good old 80/20 rule: if we can satisfy 80% of the requirements within the near 20% of the foreseeable product roadmap, we are in good shape. Otherwise, we should probably continue to shop around.

Putting aside the unhealthy imbalance between product and engineering (hey - we have Streams now!), the second takeaway is that if you do not have a way to change fundamental aspects of the component you are starting from, you should be looking for a different option. If there is a chance that you would need to make fundamental changes in the near or further future, you should look for a starting point that you could mold as your own.

So, you don't start from scratch; as we've discussed, you have the ownership and capacity to introduce fundamental changes to the piece you are integrating. You should be at a level where you could change things from their foundation, and the best way to do it is to have access to the code. Plenty of excellent open-source options allow that; if not, there are ways to build that capacity into your licensing agreement.

There's another aspect here for having access to the source code: You can learn from it! When you dive into the code to change it, you need to understand how it drives the functionality; doing so can provide an exceptional learning experience. In addition, you get to look into the developer's mind and have an imaginary dialog with them: "why did you write it like that?" You can use your judgment; if you like it - learn from it, and if you don't like it - change it!

The chance to get a feel for the code, to observe and understand it, is when the mutation aspect comes into play. A mutation starts with connecting with the source of that which you are changing. It stems from apprehending how it was built and designed, the thinking behind it, and the assumptions and compromises made. There is enormous learning potential with all of this. And so, when you understand it, you can change it. It is the essence of mutating. It is profound and does not come from knowing how things behave on the surface. It comes from understanding how it works from its core.

ITERATE: MINIMAL VIABLE CHANGE

The facet of iteration is crucial as well. The idea is not to revolutionize or introduce many changes at once. Instead, we are trying to evolve by making small and manageable modifications frequently and continuously. I call such a change a Minimal Viable Change. There is no clear-cut way to define this term; it is more about developing a feeling for it, and we can use a few guidelines to help us get there.

Before we discuss these guidelines, let's first set the premise. The thinking behind MVC is similar to the concept of a Minimal Viable Product – an approach that has gained so much popularity and success that it now seems almost natural. We adopt the essence of this concept and apply it at a smaller scale, the scale of a feature. Similar concept, different scale, self-similarity over scale – fractals again!

ProductPlan.com defines Minimal Viable Product as "a product with enough features to attract early-adopter customers and validate a product idea early in the product development cycle. In industries such as software, the MVP can help the product team receive user feedback as quickly as possible to iterate and improve the product.".

In his Lean Startup methodology, Eric Reis describes the purpose of an MVP as *"the version of a new product that allows a team to collect the maximum amount of validated learning about customers with the least amount of effort."* – we are trying to apply similar thinking at a smaller scale of a product feature.

Now, with a better understanding of what an MVC is, we can continue with providing a few guidelines for applying this concept: The first guideline is that the change should introduce an improvement or at least an intended improvement, which could take the form of added functionality, performance improvement, a modification that uses resources more efficiently, or more straightforward code or even documentation.

A Minimal Viable Change should be quick to implement and deploy, and typically a complete life cycle from ideation to production should be between hours to a few days. The final characteristic of a Minimal Viable Change is that its deployment is reversible with minimal risk or disruption to service delivery - the flow must go on!

CHAPTER SEVEN – MOVEMENT AND FLOW

The next pillar we shall discuss is an important one, and it has to do with the challenge of **keeping members of our organization interested, engaged, motivated, and energized**. We are looking for a way to keep their capacity to continue influencing, learning, and evolving within our organization. How do we achieve that? Through movement.

MOVEMENT AND TRANSFORMATION ARE INTRINSIC

Movement, flow, and transformation are intrinsic to life processes in nature. With shifting wind patterns, churning ocean currents, and massive bird migrations, our world is constantly on the move. These processes play a key role in regulating climate and species survival. The true scale of such movements is impossible to capture with the naked eye. However, with big data techniques used to create wind maps and GPS tracking used to map migrating birds, dynamic visualizations capture the magnitude of movement in various natural phenomena. Whatever is not moving, whatever's not flowing, ultimately decays.

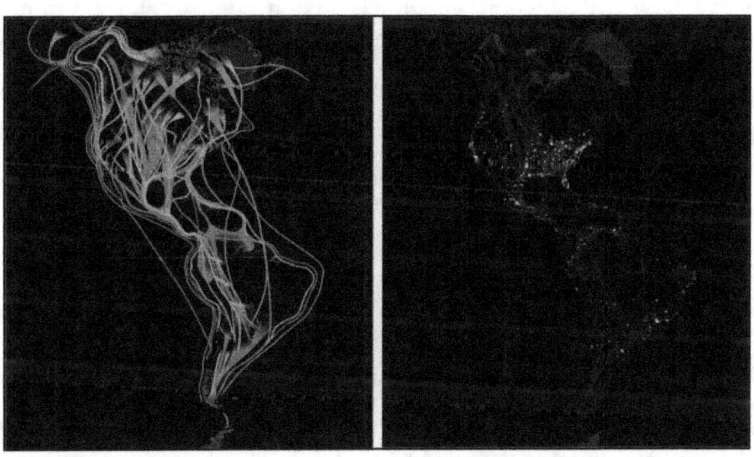

Bird migration in the Americas – A visualization.[xxxi]

75

Working in an organization is like being in a relationship; after the initial excitement and high level of intensity, we transition into a steady state. The flow and overall energy diminish at that point, and passion weakens.

This steady state becomes a risk for both the organization and the employees. However, both parties have put much energy into getting to this point and are vested in maintaining a positive relationship and a high level of engagement, motivation, energy, and contribution.

MOVEMENT WITHIN THE STREAM

So how do we begin? The first way we achieve movement in our organization of streams is within streams. Earlier, we discussed the stream as a quantum of value delivery, and there are two to seven members in a stream. Each member can perform all the aspects of value delivery that the stream produces. However, at least one of the members is always more knowledgeable in one or more areas than the others. And so, to accomplish movement within a stream, we rotate the areas of expertise and proficiency among the members. Pretty straightforward but not always easy to do.

For example, if one member is the expert on production aspects or what we now call DevOps: pipeline, version control, and environment management at one point in time, then that expertise, over time, would be passed to another team member through mentorship, knowledge sharing, and working closely together on tasks from that domain. Ultimately, when the proficiency of the mentored member is sufficient, they can become the "designated" expert in that domain.

The idea is to achieve movement by interchanging domain expertise between stream members. Of course, it would be up to the stream to orchestrate these transitions. Still, the main thing is that this internal movement and flow is practiced, and we do not end up in stagnation where the internal structure of the streams, in terms of subject matter expertise, does not change over time. That would have a counter effect and, unfortunately, is the norm for so many software teams.

An interesting anecdote I would like to share in this context is from my recent experience being involved in growing vegetables on a small local farm not far from where I live. I have been involved in the practice of "Crop Rotation", which is the practice of systematically moving various crops around a garden to maintain soil fertility. It turns out that by rotating crops from one spot to another each season, you can preserve and even boost the nutrients in the soil. I won't go into the science behind this, but remarkably, a similar concept of movement and rotation is common to completely different domains. Contemplating the correspondence of benefits between the two and how you can explain one in terms of another can be an excellent exercise for understanding the deep meaning of movement within a stream and why it is so essential that we incorporate it into our practice.

MOVEMENT ACROSS STREAMS

The second type of movement and flow is across streams. Again, the streams remain constant in terms of their essence or functional boundaries within the organization. Let's say there is a stream that handles the user management aspect of the application we provide. The stream handles the functional aspects of managing users, authentication, profile management, provisioning, permissions, roles, etc.

Let's assume that this stream has three or four members; over time, these members will likely exhaust their overall ability to be engaged, interested, energized, and influence change and advancement. This is only natural; over time, we settle into a steady state and retreat into our comfort zone and familiarity.

Sadly, this inevitably affects our performance, and the various measures and KPIs will likely drop. Having movement of members across the stream helps individuals step out of their comfort zone and into a growth zone.

EXAMPLE OF HENRY FORD

Let's look at another example of movement and how it is leveraged to scale; this example is from the beginning of the previous century, and it is a production technique invented by Henry Ford. Innovation was a way of life for Henry Ford. Like today, innovators of the past challenged the status quo and created a reality that did not exist before. They started with new ideas, sometimes their own, sometimes others, and grew and nurtured those ideas until they became an accepted part of daily life. While Ford did not invent the modern automobile, he did invent a technique for mass-producing automobiles and scale manufacturing.

Interestingly enough, this technique involved movement, revolutionizing the automobile industry and the concept of scaled manufacturing worldwide. Ford invented the moving assembly line that allowed Model T parts to flow through the stream and sub-streams of the assembly process. The assembly line consisted of multiple stations, and the car's chassis moved along the assembly line stations where workers trained to work at those stations would apply their assigned parts to the chassis. Sheer production of the Model T dramatically scaled, and the production time for a single car dropped by a big factor. These concepts allowed Ford to increase their profit margin and lower the cost of the vehicle to consumers.

While the assembly line technique simplified the production process and increased capacity, employee turnover was a serious challenge and had an adverse effect on the assembly line approach. Workers found the assembly line work boring and repetitive; they now had to do several simple tasks instead of building an entire vehicle. Ford solved this challenge partly with his $5 workday program; however, repetitive and mundane tasks have been an ongoing challenge in the manufacturing industry ever since. No system is a perfect one.

In a study focused on human factors in industrial production systems[xxxii], Michaela Dalle Mura and Gino Dini proposed an organizational strategy to move workers periodically among line stations, thus reducing monotony and improving ergonomics.

While software delivery is very different from industrial production, there are some common challenges. The rotation of roles within a stream and the movement of stream members across different streams are similar to the rotation of workers among line stations and offer similar benefits.

By rotating members between streams, we expose them to other areas of our solutions; we help them gain additional perspectives on our product verticals and learn new functional facets of the industry to which we offer solutions.

Remember that streams are autonomous in terms of their technologies, culture, processes, and so forth. So, by rotating members across streams, we encourage them to become familiar with other types of technologies, different approaches, and the diversity of cultures. We keep them engaged and interested; we seamlessly introduce new goals, environments, and technologies.

And we do all of that while retaining them in our organization. They meet new people and become familiar with more aspects of the application we deliver. We help them grow within the organization naturally and in a healthy way. The benefit for the organization is that we can retain our members, retain knowledge, gain high energy levels of productivity, and deliver value over time.

CHAPTER EIGHT – SCALE AND SELF-REGULATION

In this chapter, we will be discussing the pillar that **controls scale**. This book is about scaling software delivery, and it is time we present the pillar that addresses the essence of scaling delivery in its most fundamental way. In previous chapters, we introduced the stream as a quantum of software delivery; we talked about the stream being autonomous and saw how autonomy was a facet of Liberty, which is also a fundamental stream characteristic.

However, having liberty and autonomy does not mean that streams operate independently. Streams communicate and interact (we will discuss this in greater detail in the "Direction and Alignment" pillar). Streams are also interconnected and form a fractal structure that drives scale.

BRANCHING

Let's dive in then and see how we drive and control scale within the DevStream paradigm. The process that drives scale is called *Branching*. A few scenarios merit branching: the most common is when we need to scale up. A scale-up is required when the desired throughput from the stream surpasses its capacity, and the stream is already at its member cap (seven). Measuring capacity and throughput are not straightforward, but fortunately, we don't need to measure them directly. We can look for where the stream throughput reaches its peak and will start to decline, and we identify this point by tracking KPI trends.

The KPIs we track will depend on the stream's development methodology; if we embrace all the DevStream pillars, we can focus on Minimal Viable Change as a KPI driver. Minimal Viable Change is a concept we discussed in depth in the Integrate, Mutate, and Iterate pillar and is a set of modifications that go through a complete delivery cycle from ideation through development to production. Minimal Viable Change sets are deployed frequently and continuously. We can measure and track their delivery frequency and use this frequency as the KPI we track over time to identify trends.

We define the MVC delivery frequency as the average of MVC cycles delivered by a stream during a fixed time frame, typically two or four weeks. We then track the mean MVC cycles on a quarterly or bi-quarter basis and can identify trends over time. When we notice a consistent decline trend in this KPI, it usually indicates that we have surpassed the delivery capacity for the stream and should consider branching.

If we practice a different software development methodology, we can use a subset of the accepted measures to track performance for that methodology. For example, if we practice Agile, we can track Velocity, Sprint Burndown, Cycle Time, and other trends, then look for when they peak and subsequently decline.

Regardless of the development methodology used, remember that a stream drives the entire set of services and resources in software delivery; this means QA, DevOps, and customer care. We can track prevalent KPI trends in those domains and identify their peak points as indicators for when we are at capacity for the stream delivery capability. Does that make sense?

When the member count of the stream is at maximum, there is another way to sense when a *scale-up branching* is needed; this way does not involve KPIs or numbers but relies on **our feeling of pressure**. We have all been there and know how pressure feels, which usually means we are at capacity. But how do we know when we've reached that point? When it is the collective feeling of Stream members that the overall work pressure they are experiencing is ongoing over an extended period and is a risk to their well-being and performance, then we are at a point where branching is merited.

I believe that pressure is a driver for branching in nature as well, and when the overall pressure of flow exceeds a specific limit within a river stream, it will branch from the "parent" stream. Branching can also occur when it is evident that additional scoped functionality will not fit into the stream. It could be a new planned module, a new vertical to consider, or a large set of added use cases we need to deliver.

And so, let's say we have reached the point where we need to scale up. What's the process? We perform branching by splitting a sub-stream from the stream that is at capacity. The new sub-stream can be smaller in terms of its member count than the stream it split from or have the same number of members (this means we would need to grow as an organization or absorb these members from other streams if they are not at capacity).

Depending on circumstances, the new split sub-stream can have some of the original members of the stream it split from as its "founding" members, or it can be comprised of a completely new team. This is where the fundamental concept of "there are no rules" comes into play again for the structure and characteristics of the new sub-stream. Ideally, the facets of the Liberty pillar should also apply, so it is up to the new stream to organize itself.

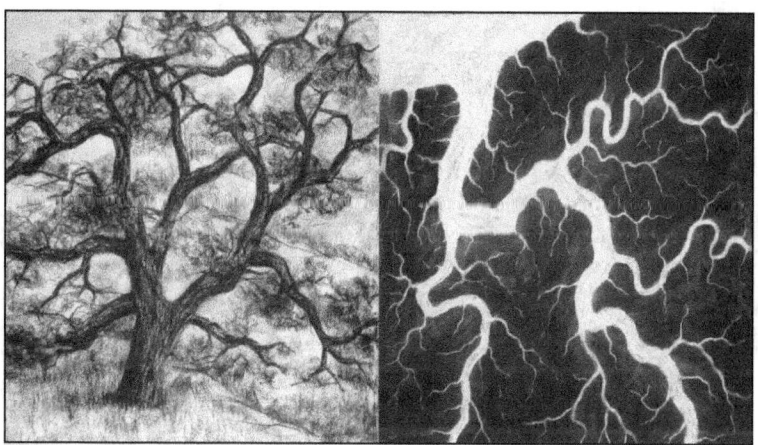

"Branching, meandering" - Peter Howells [xxxiii]

SELF-REGULATION

The flip side of scale-up and branching is self-regulation, which involves reducing stream member count and merging. I will use the term flow here as an analogy to the flow in rivers or even the flow of light. Surprisingly, physicists have discovered the phenomena of branching flow we typically see with rivers in light when it travels and propagates through a specific medium.

Flow can be an analogy to the amount of work that "flows" into or through a stream. Flow is never constant and fluctuates over time as objectives, business volume, and the performance of stream members vary. When flow diminishes and stays lower than the capacity potential of the stream for an extended period, we should assess whether there needs to be a change in the number of members of the stream or a change in its composition. When a stream's member count decreases, the members transitioning from the stream can be absorbed by other existing streams that need to grow or in new sub-streams that split and branch from over-capacity streams.

These processes of scale-up branching and self-regulation introduce flow and energy optimization. Self-regulation and branching take place at the stream level, but they drive the organization's dynamics, structure, and coherence.

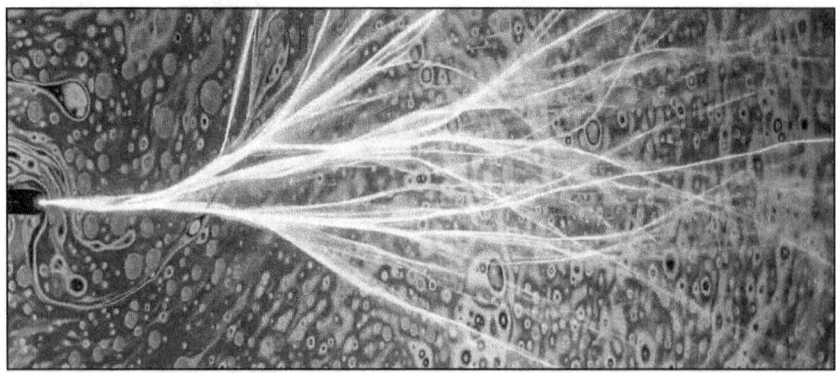

Haifa, Israel July 2, 2020 – A team of researchers from Technion – Israel Institute of Technology has observed a branched flow of light for the very first time. The findings are published in the prestigious scientific journal Nature and are presented on the cover of the July 2, 2020 issue.[xxxiv]

CHAPTER NINE – DIRECTION AND ALIGNMENT

In this pillar, we discuss how streams communicate. Streams are autonomous, but they do not operate in a void. The various streams make up our organization, and communication is critical for all streams to be aligned with the organization's goals. Communication is also needed to fulfill particular needs, address gaps or deal with challenges streams may encounter.

One of the ways to communicate between streams is through providing *Direction*. Direction is also a property of flow; after all, we are drawing our inspiration from rivers and streams!

Before we explore streams direction and alignment in more detail, I'll briefly mention that our feelings should play a role in setting direction and how we communicate them. I have mentioned in this book that I believe feelings are a form of subconscious computations that consider relevant factors and parameters; these could be based on past experiences or predictions about a possible future.

When we have a good feeling about something and contemplate doing or saying it, it usually means something internal to us has determined (through a complex computation) that it is probable to affect our future experience positively. As professionals in our work environment, we are often encouraged to push our feelings aside and focus on demonstratable facts and things we can measure. We can greatly benefit from being more aware of our feelings when setting a direction and influencing a positive outcome when we focus on the right feelings when we communicate direction. I was pleasantly surprised when researching this subject to see how much research has been done on how emotions help us achieve our goals. I will be referring to some examples later in this chapter.

In traditional software organizations, as leaders and managers, we give direction, and as team members and contributors, we usually ask for directions. I was using the word direction repeatedly here on purpose. I could have used "guidance," "advice," or "instructions", but the word "direction" sets the right tone for the atmosphere and interaction we seek in DevStreams.

When someone is lost, they ask for directions, and those who provide them with directions set them on the right path to their destination. Direction is also the course in which we communicate guidance. In DevStreams, when we, as an upstream, provide direction, we do it downstream, and when our sub-stream asks for directions, it does so upstream.

When we provide direction, we focus on the "What"; it is up to the receiving end to determine the "How." This approach ensures that we maintain the autonomy of sub-streams and embrace learning and growth opportunities. Of course, the sub-stream can always request guidance, clarifications, or more concrete directions if needed from the upstream. So ultimately, there is an ongoing and bi-directional dialog between streams while maintaining autonomy and a distinct path for initiative, goal setting, and growth.

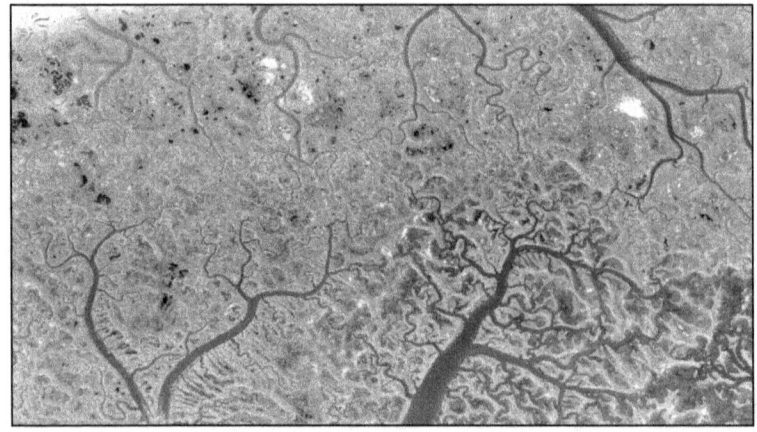

The Natural Fractals of Google Earth. Spain [xxxv]

Regarding how direction is given downstream, it would typically be at a high level - what we are not doing is we are not managing other streams, and a down-stream is not an execution arm of an upstream. We are not introducing an organizational hierarchy; we suggest the direction in which value grows and how we address gaps in knowledge and guidance.

Observing nature, there is no apparent hierarchy seen, but patterns allow for scaled flow and effective energy management. For our purposes, we are trying to mimic a similar structure to achieve effective communication and flow of knowledge. When we want to direct our sub-stream in terms of what we need, we should provide them with high-level goals, and these goals and strategies will then be translated into a set of actions and tactics by the sub-stream.

PROVIDING DIRECTION, THE RIGHT WAY

In DevStreams, the inherent anatomy of streams and the primal characteristics of autonomy and accountability allow us to distinguish between providing direction and giving directions almost naturally. Nailing down *direction* is only the first step. We want direction to inspire greatness and do that using our imagination.

A famous quote by Albert Einstein says: *"Imagination is more important than knowledge. For knowledge is limited, whereas Imagination embraces the entire world, stimulating progress, giving birth to evolution"*. We should encourage streams to use imagination when giving direction. In their paper from 1999, "Towards a New Model of Strategy-making as Serious Play," Roos and Victor introduce three types of imagination: descriptive, creative, and challenging, claiming the fourth type of imagination, strategic imagination is an emergent property of a complex interplay between the three.

TYPES OF IMAGINATION

Descriptive imagination helps us grasp abstract concepts by transforming the abstract into tangible through a cognitive process. Using our words or drawings, we can describe and create a mental picture that captures the essence of the abstract concept and allows us to implement it. According to Dr. Shai Hershkovits in his "Imagining Strategy: Using Imagination in Strategic Planning" article, this type of imagination is associated with patterns and regularities identification from large quantities of information and data. Individuals with an imagination of this type can identify challenges and opportunities, make sense of them, and form a strategy.

The next type of imagination is *creative imagination*, commonly called "out-of-the-box" thinking. Creative imagination goes beyond describing an existing abstract reality and enables us to construct a new reality, leading to innovation and advancement to bridge the gap between what exists now and what we imagine.

Then there is *challenging imagination*. Dr. Shai Hershkovit's article states: "challenging imagination stands in contrast to the other two. With challenging imagination, we criticize, challenge, and sometimes even destroy what was achieved by way of the previous two.

This is the kind of imagination that undermines all previous rules and assumptions and provides a clear cognitive playground to test the unthinkable. It doesn't presuppose anything, and it doesn't use previous knowledge as a given. It simply starts everything from scratch. It deconstructs existing knowledge, perception, and language. It uses cynicism and sarcasm and sees nothing as sacred."

"The tree which moves some to tears of joy is in the eyes of others only a green thing that stands in the way. Some see Nature as all ridicule and deformity... and some scarce see Nature at all. But to the eyes of the man

of Imagination, Nature is Imagination itself." – William Blake, poet and painter.

And so, we can turn to nature to practice and expand our imagination. As children, we all heavily use our imagination when playing in a natural environment. Children use imagination to correlate objects and structures they see in a natural setting and those that influence their reality from stories or other facets of their daily experiences. They see dragons and castles in trees, play with wooden sticks as if they were swords, and spot cotton candy in a cloud formation.

With time and age, we become more "realistic"; we lose our naivety and use our imagination less when observing and experiencing nature. But this can be changed. We appreciate the ingenuity of nature and can use our imagination to correlate between structures, processes, and behaviors we observe in nature and concepts, ideas, and patterns from our professional daily experiences.

We are all familiar with the term "World Wide Web" and can appreciate the correlation between the structure of a spider web and the topology of a worldwide network of networks. Any software engineer is familiar with the tree data structure and can appreciate the correlation between the abstract data structure and a natural tree.

This is something we can exercise daily to extend our imagination. When we are working and notice a data pattern, try to correlate it to a similar pattern found in nature. When we analyze a process or design a user experience, maybe something in nature triggers our memory and invokes our imagination.

Similarly, when we are outdoors and experience nature, we can look for similarities in our work experience. Cloud formations, landscape topography, colors, sounds, we experience it all and can contemplate how we can correlate them with concepts and experiences from our work.

Nature re-uses structures, geometries, and processes across multiple domains and systems.

Another fun exercise is to notice where nature applies a structure or process, you are familiar with in a different context. For example, in the following picture, we can use our imagination and see how the structures of a branching river and riverbanks are formed within a cloud formation.

A cloud-covered part of Earth, photographed from the International Space Station.[xxxvi]

THE WHAT AND THE HOW

One of the guidelines we mentioned for direction is to focus on the "what" instead of the "how." However, when we communicate direction, the "How" becomes important. By conveying direction with the right emotion or feeling, we increase the chances of a successful outcome. David DeSteno, a professor of psychology at Northwestern University and editor-in-chief of the journal Emotion, in his article "Three Emotions That Can Help You Succeed at Your Goals," proposes we cultivate the positive emotions of Gratitude, Compassion, and Pride.

According to DeSteno, these three emotions evolved to help us act effortlessly in kind and helpful ways. Because the strength of these emotions does not wane after repeated use, they have an advantage over reason, habits, and willpower. In research done by DeSteno, he was able to demonstrate how stimulating gratitude affects behavior. Those who had experienced gratitude in one of the experiments and were asked to help another person with a project that involved working on hard problems volunteered to persevere with the problems longer, despite not being watched or paid.

A GRATITUDE JOURNAL

DeSteno proposes keeping a gratitude journal, logging things we are grateful for a few times a week as a practice for increasing our gratitude. Compassion is caring about others without receiving a reward; it has demonstrated positive effects on the type of self-control that stops the normal tit-for-tat that causes people to lose out in the long run. [xxxvii]

Pride can also help us achieve our goals, as long as it does not turn into hubris. DeSteno's article states: "*Pride is a natural response to successfully accomplishing your goals and being recognized by others for your abilities. When it is authentic, it signals to others that you are a capable and reliable person, which is how it evolved in the first place—as a way to raise one's status in a group. People with greater authentic pride tend to attain their goals and have higher self-control.*"

COMPLEX NETWORKS

Direction is not the only way streams communicate. In nature, we can find examples of complex networks that enable communications between birds and insects, microorganisms, plants, and trees. Let's explore a few before we continue discussing communication between streams. The first example is evidence that trees communicate via an underground network of fungal connections - this type of network has come to be known as the 'wood-wide web.' It turns out that neighboring plants exchange nutrients, sugars, water, and more through the intertwined web of roots and fungi than we ever thought they did. By staying connected, plants can provide mutual support and help shape the ecosystem they inhabit. Wow!

Bacteria can perform complex collective actions, although they are simple organisms. They leverage a mechanism called 'quorum sensing' to achieve coordination, allowing them to colonize hosts and defend against competitors. Starlings fly in huge flocks or murmurations and form breathtaking patterns as they swoop, dive, and wheel through the sky in perfect synchrony. They retain heat energy and gain protection from predators by gathering in numbers. The individuals stay coordinated as a group by following their seven closest neighbors and moving accordingly. They follow simple rules to create complex patterns.

As such, streams communicate with their neighboring streams to align on goals, exchange knowledge, and support one another. They often share the same application domain or business context and have much to communicate. This type of communication will be less structured and based more on the interaction around areas of operation, various milestones accomplished, lessons learned, and challenges or gaps overcome.

Starlings murmuration.[xxxviii]

EPILOGUE – THOUGHTS ON NEXT STEPS

This is where your journey with DevStreams begins! In this book, I have tried to take inspiration from nature and apply ideas to a field I am familiar with. Nature evolves by introducing small steps, and I believe we should do the same.

For those of you who wish to practice the paradigm as a whole, I would suggest starting small and experimenting with a dedicated team that is open to new ideas and is aligned with the overall theme of the paradigm.

For those who find ideas presented in this book compelling but are hesitant to apply them as a new practice, I would say pick one or two ideas and focus on implementing them in your operation. I believe that as you start exploring this path, you will likely advance to implement more and more ideas that will get you closer to practicing the entire paradigm on an ongoing basis.

And for those who are still skeptical, I hope you at least found the reading of this book interesting and, over time, contemplate some of the ideas to the point where you can mold and change them into something you feel comfortable experimenting with and benefitting from in your operation.

I'll sign off with a quote I came across recently: *"Nature is never in a hurry, yet it accomplishes all."*

Brilliant.

Thank you for reading!

END NOTES

i Illustration by Eric Taylor, Woods Hole Oceanographic Institution
source: https://www.whoi.edu/press-room/news-release/river-carbon/

ii Image: Dennis Chesters—NASA GOES Project/Goddard Space Flight Center

iiihttp://commons.wikimedia.org/wiki/File:Mangere_Inlet_Fractal_Patterns_In_Mudflats

iv https://artfulmath.com/fractal-patterns-in-nature/

v https://phys.org/news/2008-12-rivers-gas-stars-space-image.html

vi https://www.toolsqa.com/agile/agile-methodology/

vii https://en.wikipedia.org/wiki/Diminishing_returns

viii Source: https://climate.nasa.gov/climate_resources/67/lena-delta-russia/

ix Source: www.researchgate.net/figure/Self-similarity-of-Mandelbrot-set-in-different-scales_fig1_342374134

x Source: www.crops.org/about-crops/biology

xi Source: https://naturebackin.com/2020/12/04/patterns-in-nature-fractals/

xii Source: https://www.artfido.com/amazing-photographs-of-fractals-in-nature/

xiii Source: http://time.com/3791692/finding-beauty-fractal-patterns-on-earth-as-seen-from-space/

xiv Source: https://www.artfido.com/amazing-photographs-of-fractals-in-nature/

xv https://biomimicry.org/what-is-biomimicry/

xvi https://biomimicry.org/janine-benyus/

xvii https://asknature.org/innovation/high-speed-train-inspired-by-the-kingfisher/

xviii Source: https://www.bloomberg.com/news/articles/2008-02-11/using-nature-as-a-design-guidebusinessweek-business-news-stock-market-and-financial-advice

xix https://youmatter.world/en/definition/definitions-what-is-biomimicry-definition-examples/

xx https://biomimicry.org/what-is-biomimicry/

xxi https://builtin.com/artificial-intelligence

xxii https://lupinepublishers.com/material-science-journal/fulltext/what-is-quantum-computing-and-how-it-works-artificial-intelligence-driven-by-quantum-computing.ID.000157.php

xxiii https://techdayhq.com/community/articles/how-blockchain-technology-is-shattering-everything-from-banks-to-healthcare

xxiv Source: https://www.nasa.gov/image-feature/lake-of-the-ozarks-in-missouri

xxv www.sciencephoto.com/media/325999/view/rivers-on-mars

xxvi Source:www.aci-iac.ca/my-canada-my-art-history/dr-samantha-nutt-on-colorado-river-delta-2-by-edward-burtynsky/

xxvii Source: en.wikipedia.org/wiki/Fractal-generating_software

xxviii Source: time.com/3791692/finding-beauty-fractal-patterns-on-earth-as-seen-from-space/

xxix Source: phys.org/news/2017-03-fractal-patterns-nature-art-aesthetically.html

xxx Source: ncbi.nlm.nih.gov/pmc/articles/PMC7052590/figure/F0001/

xxxi Source:https://cartographicperspectives.org/index.php/journal/article/view/1510/1687

xxxii Dalle Mura, M., Dini, G. Job rotation and human–robot collaboration for enhancing ergonomics in assembly lines by a genetic algorithm. Int J Adv Manuf Technol 118, 2901–2914 (2022). https://doi.org/10.1007/s00170-021-08068-1

xxxiii http://www.peterhowells.com/branching-meandering-2010/

xxxiv https://www.technion.ac.il/en/2020/07/see-the-light/

xxxv Photo: Paul Bourke/Google Earth fractals, source: https://www.atlasobscura.com/articles/the-natural-fractals-of-google-earth

xxxvi https://climatekids.nasa.gov/cloud-climate/

xxxvii Dreber, A., Rand, D., Fudenberg, D. et al. Winners don't punish. Nature 452, 348–351 (2008)

xxxviii https://www.worldphoto.org/vi/node/4533

www.ingramcontent.com/pod-product-compliance
Lightning Source LLC
Chambersburg PA
CBHW070408220526
45467CB00001B/507